I'm Not Afraid of the Monsters

Rivka

Mental Illness, Madness, & MONSTERS

RIVKA M. STIEH

I'M NOT AFRAID OF THE MONSTERS
Copyright © 2021 by Rivka M. Stieh

All rights reserved. Printed in the United States of America. No part of this book may be used or reproduced in any manner whatsoever without written permission except in the case of brief quotations embodied in critical articles or reviews.

For permission contact:
Rivka.stieh@outlook.com
Or www.rivkamstieh.com

ISBN: 979-8-7546207-5-9

First Edition: November 2021

TRIGGER WARNING

    This book includes possible triggers regarding suicide, domestic violence, sexual abuse, sexual assault, addiction, and the use of profanity. This is not an entire list of other contents that may be triggering to others.

    This book is recommended for ages 18+.

Thank you to my family, most of all my children. Without them, I would have never poured my heart and soul out to the world so that another parent can be armed with knowledge and support to raise children while balancing mental illness.

To my mother, our relationship and love grows like a fine wine, assenting into something more exceptional and sophisticated with age. To my husband, my monster slayer, through it all, you press on with unconditional love.

To lifelong friendships that never wavered.

Tiffany, our pizza and wine nights never failed to band-aid any season through humor and lightheartedness.

And to all the therapists I quit. I heard you.

Contents

Preface..i
Introduction..v
ONE 1
TWO 9
THREE 17
FOUR 21
FIVE 33
SIX 37
SEVEN 43
EIGHT 47
NINE 51
TEN 59
ELEVEN 67
TWELVE 81
THIRTEEN 89
FOURTEEN 93
FIFTEEN 105
SIXTEEN 137
SEVENTEEN 147

EIGHTEEN	179
NINTEEN	181
TWENTY	185
TWENTY ONE	189
A Note from the Author	193

PREFACE

I have been asked numerous times: What story do I have to offer you, the reader? How is my story more significant than any of the others? Well, it's not. But as long as mental health, particularly that of bipolar disorder, is misunderstood, feared, ignored, and judged unfairly, every person like me has a relevant story. No bipolar patient experiences it the same way; each of us unique. It's important to give value to each book, essay, blog, or article so it may resonate with those who find similarities.

On a personal level, this book means an explanation. Just today I sat with my two daughters over lunch, reveling in my oldest' s upcoming wedding, when I said, "I'll have to lose a little weight." Her response provoked immediate illumination to the overlooked consequences of their past with me: a mother with profound body shaming issues both of environmental and biologically produced trauma. Mania-induced bulimia and depression-induced binging were a crude dance of coexistence much of my life. "Mom, stop saying that. I've literally heard you complain about your body my entire life. You have two daughters here that look just like you. How do you think that makes us feel? Be body positive."

And another source of contention with my adult daughter, which she shares with her younger sister, is that I commonly purged her room as a child. "No emotional attachments here," she mocked me. To which I replied, "I couldn't help it. No really, I couldn't help it." My physical environment has always been a huge trigger for me in any state of my disease, catapulting me into compulsive cleaning benders, including the purging of old or unused toys, screaming over clutter, and the mantra "if you can't pack your room in one box you have too many things." Many of these types of behaviors didn't generate much thought about their physical or emotional attachments.

My daughter is unapologetically honest. Her soul still carries the pain that life with me caused her. She's navigating adulthood, her love for me, and what that should look like, while processing the trauma she is carrying. And desperately looking for a way to unload it. I owe this book to her and her siblings. To try and understand through my words what being bipolar felt like raising them. Ideally, I hope for some enlightenment through the narration of my mind and monster. Some glimmer of intention that offers an `ounce of validation of my love for them.

On a larger scale, this book means empathy and compassion. Bipolar disorder doesn't discriminate between race, gender, socio-economic status, or demographic. You could be selected to speak with Michelle Obama at a university on the subject of women and the economy or have Barack Obama narrate your life in an infomercial. Been raised by a senator bumping elbows with well-known politicians.

Traveled across the globe or had just about every opportunity at your feet. All of these things happened to me. Yet with bipolar disorder, you end up so far removed from your natural intellect, lifestyle, or life calling that you don't recognize the person you've become. I owe it to everyone like me to explain what this demise looks like.

A formidable lifelong brawl of two forces vying for dominance. The monster and its plot to establish an equilibrium of ups and downs, and the host, one's conscious and subconscious, trying to stay present to get from one day to the next. All parallel to any external factors adding fuel to the already ignited fire in the brain. I have battled just that scenario all my life. From being born under violent circumstances, an honorary member of the #metoo movement, crime, domestic violence, verbal abuse, joining the Army on a manic whim leaving my children behind, multiple marriages, seasonally based unmedicated bipolar domination, suicidal ideation to suicidal planning, a vicious attack under psychosis, and hospitalization. To adequate care, intense therapy, spirituality, love, and finally self-acceptance.

This book is dark, it's painful, it's enlightening, and through the pages of my journals, poems, and essays of my life, you can see me as a real, raw human being who deserves dignity, redemption, understanding, and grace for an illness that deserves continued study. I hope these pages find their way into the hands of mothers and fathers, brothers and sisters, husbands and wives, teachers and caregivers, pastors and rabbis who share a common denominator of one person in their life who needs your full commitment to the comprehension of this relentless but manageable disease.

The following is a non-linear outline of events as I, the author, recall them. Some names and places have been changed to protect their privacy.

INTRODUCTION

In the dark season, it is a fight between good and evil, energy and weakness, impulsiveness and indifference. My brain is home to an alternate universe, a pitch-black, spine-chilling compartment housing entirely dark monsters with no distinguishable features. They rip from my amygdala and shred my prefrontal cortex. A complicated battle that carries on with varying degrees of frequency and intensity

The monsters, much like the Devil, are not omnipresent, but their chaos most certainly is. The darkness is created internally by biologically and environmentally fractured, tattered, and weak souls. They leave behind a fog of melancholy that imprisons the cerebrum, perpetuating insanity. They are woven into my psyche, whispering vile wickedness into my frontal lobe, and I think it's truth. When the fog alternates in density, I grasp traces of enlightened cognitive responses amidst significant cognitive impairment. A subconscious warrior transmitting unconscious communication as subtle, intuitive tugs.

RIVKA M. STIEH

I am in control, no matter the toll
Let it begin, you will not win
The dark season is here
But I have no fear
For I have an indestructible soul
~ Rivka

ONE

The Fated Fall

I always carried a weighted blanket of financial strain, career inadequacies, a burdensome living arrangement, and riding on the edges of every compounding inconvenience. My emotions were heightened, and I questioned the universe. How could I possibly endure anymore?

The low tire gauge light screamed at me from the dash of my car, as it had four times that week. It was a personal assault to my sanity. Even as innocuous as it seems, it was the tip of a breaking point. My skin was on fire with anger at the mere nuisance factor of having to pull over at yet another gas station. An internal dialogue of disgust ensued on repeat. "If you had your finances in order, you could just buy a new tire—or fuck, a new car!"

During this internal discord I forcefully pulled the obnoxiously tangled air hose to my tire connecting the air nozzle and valve stem. Overwhelmed with agitation, I used sight perception to scale the tire's fullness, mostly looking away with revulsion instead of competently monitoring its completeness. Gaining a little composure with a breeze flowing past my face, I look to the tire. In that mere millisecond of motion, my face to tire, it detonated, a remarkable airburst putting out an impactful bang. Dust particles bounced off my skin like miniscule pieces of glass. And everything stopped.

The world was suddenly silent, followed by a faint ringing in my ears. I tried to stand tall, robotically composed, blank in thought, eyes wide open, and dazed. Glassy and subtlety regaining some acuity. Haphazardly looking for my cell phone. I had some awareness that I needed it. When my fingers met with my phone, I placed it to my ear, then mustered the wherewithal to call a friend for help. Upon his arrival everything was still vague and muffled in my mind. There was some small talk while he removed the blown tire carcass, replacing it for the small, temporary spare. I struggled to gesture appreciation for his aid. I found it difficult to bring words to lips through an increasing psychosis.

Seeing his brake lights and left turn signal followed by the minimization of his truck bed provided a sense of relief. I then sat behind the wheel of my red Ford Focus gripping it and contemplating what to do next. The brain fog was still significantly in attendance. I was not even sure my brain was intentionally telling my hands to hold the steering wheel or my feet to use the gas and brakes. A form of autopilot and muscle memory got me in the direction of my home. My remembrance of that twelve minutes from the Finish Line Gas Station to the gravel road that met my driveway is spotty. As if my eyes were opening and closing in slow motion, leaving blanks in memory.

I'M NOT AFRAID OF THE MONSTERS

I arrived mindlessly disengaged from emotions but with an awareness of the things that had created some discontents. I walked into my home with these loose thoughts regarding the stressful imperfections my home caused me. I recalled how I often despised pulling into the driveway and had to compose myself to go inside this one-hundred-year-old, patchworked farmhouse. I abhorred the incomplete and disorganized mudroom, black stick tile crumbling in corners, a sagging floorboard at the threshold, a yellow-stained hole with a lone strip of ceiling hanging above, and the dirt clinging to the textured white walls and overpainted window trim.

This led into the aged kitchen through an old door that either wouldn't close or wouldn't open, which preset dark wood floors that sank when you walked on them in some places. The house featured do-it-yourself attempts to create some resemblance of a more modern décor, along with galvanized rippled metal as the backsplash, followed by different pieces and sizes of cabinets put together and hand-painted dark gray. This was aligned with Home Goods pieces creating a faux romantic farmhouse feel. I had been feeling that all the work my husband and I had done to date felt a lot like walking helplessly upstream of whitewater rapids.

Environmental chaos creates internal chaos. The state of my home should be the one thing I can actually control. I acknowledge I am to be grateful to have a roof over my head. And I do. But this mind, these monsters, my hypersensitive-driven thought process makes every out-of-sort line, pile of things, furniture, dirt, array of books, unmade bed, closet, and picture on the wall a manic frenzy. It creates an anxious, uneasy agitation building in my chest, presenting as crying, screaming, pacing, then feverish cleaning. All amplified by people who don't share my need for order.

Sometimes chaos is followed by defeat, sadness, fatigue, an inability to muster any bother to clean up, and order is completely lost again. I engage my surroundings further: the presence of life in the living room, unfolded blankets, an unvacuumed floor, dog toys, ball caps, cups, video game cases, or shoes. In our bedroom, boots, a wallet, a flashlight, papers, or work items are chaotically arranged on my husband's side of the bed.

After noting my disdain for the living arrangements, I dispassionately sit at the end of my bed thinking about what I should to do to regain control and alleviate the pressures. I'm surprisingly clear and calculated in my directive now. I take a quick call from my brother-in-law, who proceeds to remind me my marriage is in upheaval because of all the changes my husband made on my behalf, and the ones I didn't make for him.

My husband is a southern country guy through and through, avid hunter, gun connoisseur, homegrown, home-cooked meal eating, boot wearing, cowboy hat dawning, "ma'am" and "sweetheart" spouting, rough, loyal, religious, and simple man. Whereas I, a city woman, am used to upper class accommodations, minimalist, vegan, Jewish, senator's daughter, liberal, flying by the seat of my pants, and predictably unpredictable.

The phone call, the clutter, climbing resentment, anger, guilt, and an unexpressed but acknowledged rage is cultivating deeper. It comes to me; I know what I have to do now. It needs to be swift and without error. I obtained my husband's pistol, the one under his side of the mattress, the one that has no safety. I walk outside and isolated my target. Puppeteered by my ominous friends, despondent and cold, I clench the pistol in my left hand, then my right, point to my victim, look her in the eyes, and execute ten rounds in succession to ensure my mission is complete.

Moments later, wholly awoken in terror; I feel the realization of this slaughtering. "What have I done? Make it stop, make it stop. Oh my God, what have I done!" My thoughts are rapid, inconsistent, jumbled, full of emotional flooding. I'm overloading and leading to another short-circuit. My sobs and screams consume any reasoning I'm attempting to make. I ran to the mudroom unloading the hideous weapon out of my hands, tossing it atop the dryer. I call my husband's best friend and wait outside while my emotional state continues to decline.

I must appear out of sorts when he arrives; I barely hear him. "What's going on?" he repeats. Then says my name repeatedly trying to prompt a response. My speech is erratic and drowned by hysteria as I attempt to articulate the scene. There is an increasing intensity and concern, or maybe it's fear, in the voice of my husband's friend. "Darlin', do you have the gun on you now?" For his safety and mine, he pulls me into him to both sincerely hug me and pat me down for weapons. Jay wants to comfort me, despite what I had done; it's in his nature. A true saving grace for my husband and me. A kind ear, kind home, and generous heart in times of strain. As loyal as a friend could be. I believe subconsciously that is why I chose to call him.

Emotional pain strikes my mind, with physical effects following suit. I tremble continuously. Justin calmly and gently places me in the passenger seat of his truck. "Sit right here while I go take a look." Heading up our gravel driveway he looks back to me just before stopping at the far edge of the old, gray metal outbuilding and the entrance to a pigpen and small grain silo. My sight from the front seat is limited, but I see enough of his body language. A slight pace and hand to the forehead before wearily looking back at me one more time as he disappears behind the outbuilding entirely. I have only witnessed Justin as the pillar of calm and reserve. But I can recognize the facial expressions of shock. Presumably, he is now trying to pick up my mess before anyone else sees what I have done. My daughter will be home from school soon.

He returns to the truck, and in what I think is awkward small talk, tries to get me comfortable and distracted. "Let's go sit in the kitchen and have a cup of coffee…. Darlin', did you go off your meds?... I'm always here for you; you can always come talk to me…. Everyone has moments in their lives that seem unmanageable." Jay's own wife battles with some level of mental illness, giving him some empathy for my situation. That and his friendship and love toward my husband.

Seated, he continues to ask me questions and offer insights while cautiously glancing from his phone to the front door. I am not in tune to what he is doing at first between his delicate conversation and my unintelligible cries. In what seems like a short minute, the front door to our mudroom opens followed by quick, heavy footsteps, then black boots, a black uniform, and fully equipped duty belt. My fear heightens as I look at Justin. "Darlin', I'm sorry," he says. "I had to."

Journal Entry
August 19, 2016

I end this day with indifference. I feel no connection to emotion, to my lover, to my family. I feel blank. Blankness is almost worse than fear or anger. To not feel is insanity. The monster has paralyzed me and for the time being has succeeded in numbing any real thought or emotion. And worse still, I do not fight back as I lack the desire.

TWO

Mary, Did You Know?

It may not have been the path God wanted for Mary; she was persistent in silencing His words while carving out her own trail. Fall 1974, Mary is now months into a pregnancy, growing by God's design. Life should be flourishing inside her amidst the consistent heartbeats, the rocking of her breaths in and out, and the muffled sound of her voice. These phases of development are to be an ethereal and nurturing process. One entrenched in delight and happiness anticipating the welcome of a chubby little bundle. A perfect mixture of mother and father, eager to swaddle their baby securely.

Mary's heartbeat was fast, her breaths erratic and deep, and her voice strained and loud. Violent physical altercations were thrusting her unborn child into her internal organs. Each stage of the development is rooted in piercing shocks of stress. The warmth of the amniotic fluid surrounding the tiny body is chilled by the rushes of cortisol fueling the shared bloodstream. Enzymes permanently alter the programming of a delicate brain most likely wreaking havoc on the growth process and predetermining future behaviors.

A tiny little flaw of malformed lens fibers alters the vision development. She is born slightly premature and with low birth weight, a mere five pounds. A child not welcomed and swaddled by a familiar voice to soothe the transition. Instead, whisked away by nurses to be placed into the arms of strangers. Her world disrupted by unfamiliar sounds. No moments of emotional and maternal attachment by the voice she remembers. The uncertain and insecure environment is the backdrop for this precious girl's new life.

My adoptive father: young, tall, and handsome whose tan skin, dark hair, and charming smile match his salesman-like demeanor. Unlike most men his age, he managed to dodge the Vietnam draft due to flat feet. Steve came from a faux lavish upbringing where their possessions were coveted and as bold as their wardrobes but didn't always reflect the size of their bank accounts. They loved the appeal of being among the wealthy Johnson County elite but struggled to maintain their lifestyle living beyond their means.

Steve was born to Manual, known to everyone as "Manny." He had a propensity for gambling on horses and college football and owned a business selling used cars. Steve's mother, Yetta, flaunted her dyed orange hair, gold jewelry, and fuchsia lipstick. Together they fit every typecast of a flamboyant Jewish couple from Boca Raton, Florida nestled under a cabana for the winter.

My adoptive mother hailed from Connecticut. I envisioned she was mostly naive in her cookie-cutter existence. Reminiscent of a '50s episode of *Father Knows Best*. That's not to say they didn't have some hidden-from-the-public family turmoil, because they did. My mother's father, Benjamin, a tall, goofy-looking fellow with rather large ears and a nose to match, was a successful New York accountant. He worked with some rather famous clientele comprised of a country singer-songwriter and soap opera stars.

Her mother, Muriel, a beautiful woman in her day, took care of the home and had a liking for cooking and reading. She would later publish her own Jewish cookbook. Grandma is robust in personality, stern, and to the point. She is unlike my father's parents, who were loud with personality, reflected faux decadence, and were not necessarily educated or even intelligent for that matter. Mom's parents were indeed very educated, spoke several languages, and were established and incredibly successful. They earned their money and later their piece of the American dream with an apartment in upscale Manhattan and a beach house in Greenport Long Island.

My adoptive parents met through mutual friends. Mother was taken in by Steve's ability to charm, and she wasn't the only one. He had a knack for convincing anyone to buy just about anything he was selling, including his fake personality and lines of adoration to naive women. To say he lacked a moral compass would be kind. Women to my father were simply a part of the act and what he was selling, women were buying. My mother bought it all the way to the altar. Father, into sexual exploits, drugs, fancy suits, and lavish parties, wrangled his new bride into at least temporarily negotiating her morals in an effort to be the doting wife.

By five, my parents divorced. My mom tells a story of pulling up to a stoplight in a bright orange Cadillac adorned in the most ostentatious plaid seats. Her mousy brown hair bleached blond. Oversized gold hoop earrings dangled to her neck. Topped off with freshly manicured artificial nails. As she looked at herself in the rearview mirror, she knew this wasn't the image she wanted for herself. Innately a more earthy girl, she was ashamed. This was the beginning of her identity reclamation, and we moved on to her next chapter.

The Biological Product

I can recall experiencing intense emotional outbursts or mania roughly by the age of four. It was probably due to an underlying emotional delay, unable to adequately express my feelings. I was triggered not only by the environmental chaos ensuing around me but in concert with the multitude of unintelligible chemical messages attempting to relay in my brain from an already tumultuous start.

One episode of extreme hysteria was launched over something trivial, tossing me into a crazed tantrum. I neurotically and forcefully ran a toy motorcycle back and forth, up and down the wall, unable to contain the pressure consuming my mind and body. My three-foot round body, wispy short blonde hair, and large brown eyes lost their innocent softness. My cheeks were on fire, and my blotchy skin was streaked with tears as I expelled hoarse, broken cries. Only to be further exacerbated when I realized the small insignificant toy was leaving black tire marks before me. I cried. Not the typical oh what have I done, Mom and Dad are going to be angry cry, but the screaming in a horrifying panic type of crying, an unable to catch my breath, blood-curdling, sobbing "No, Nooo, Nooo, Nooo, Nooo."

It was a response so over the top that it's ingrained in my mind. I can almost recreate the exact feelings rushing over me as if it were moments ago. It was fear, uncertainty, an overload of emotions with no controllable outlet. I was not panicking and screaming for having been sent to my room, or even the fact that I marked on the wall. My brain was dumping stress hormones as it had been accustomed since in utero into my fragile young mind for something otherwise trivial. The only way to release it was through extreme hysteria.

The hysterics and hypersensitivity increased by adding hyperactivity. I was seduced by sugar, and the drug hijacked my brain, disrupting the already disorganized communication taking place up there. My body was warmed by the rush of energy flooding through my veins within seconds of consumption. My large eyes reflected a hint of feline-like feral as the intensity radiated from my flesh. It had me so overpowered that I was unmanageable in my movements.

I physically sprinted from across the living room, pounding my head into the sofa back to feel a nanosecond of relief as the now kinetic energy moved from my head to the leather sofa back. It felt good to release it by way of this rhythmic battle. No one had any idea what really possessed my mind. It was unusual to my family. But unknowing of its origin, they laughed, entertained by my discomfort.

Just the age of three

Extreme hysteria knows no age
Something trivial inciting great craze
Neurotically and forcefully unable to contain
This tiny insignificant toy in which I play

Hypersensitivity

Dear Grandma, this sugar hijacks my faulty brain
Rushes of energy pulsing through my veins
Bouncing back and forth, my movements unmanageable
A rhythmic battle of insanity
Trying to diffuse this physical attack
You think it's funny and you kid with me
My little mind exhausted, begging you to see
That hyperactivity, I feel, has taken over me
Dear Grandma, please

THREE

Nature vs. Nurture

Nurture tends to promote the idea of familial intimacy. However, nurture, our environment, is simply the conditions in which you lived that played a part in your development, negative or positive, and the basis for much of this book. For me, nature isn't the biological component of my existence; it is a place many seek comfort. Evoking deep feelings of security. If you're religious, you may recognize how many times God sent people including Jesus to the wilderness for refuge or contemplation. Whether by God's grand design or the hand of Mother Nature and her universal forces, the wilderness, its nature, is a sanctuary and hundreds and thousands of people seek the miracle of its peacefulness every day.

Nature became relevant to me at an early age. It wasn't always a refuge, but I would come and go from its healing resources in times of growth and clarity. After my parents' divorce, there was Doug, my mother's new boyfriend. I can't recall Doug's physical appearance. It's as if in every memory I was watching him through a camera lens just out of my sight. I do know Doug was an earthy kind of guy, rugged, nothing like what I had been accustomed to. Doug taught me to recognize the distinct call of the whippoorwill, to shoot a small .22 rifle at soda cans and how to appreciate the timber around his old, rustic farmhouse. The old house was further beautified by large, billowing lilac bushes, acres of unaltered nature, with creatures so perfect they were undeniably of a higher power's design. The land was serene and quiet, and it felt safe.

As Doug taught me, I took to being a mini naturalist, drawn to the healing properties of nature anywhere I went. When my mother and Doug split, we moved to an urban-like apartment complex complete with lots of foot traffic and signs of life twenty-four hours a day. I spent many mornings pulling up every rock, every splash block on every corner of every building scouring for the common ringneck snake and pill bugs. I would load them into the pockets of my overalls and tote them home, letting them loose to play beside me on my bedroom floor.

My long blonde hair was in tangled pigtails, my clothes dirty from my recent excavations, and my round face smeared with whatever soil had remained on my hands as I rubbed loose hairs from my eyes. Even in our new surroundings, I fondly explored nature and all its elements; it had the ability to make everything else seem distant.

Single, my mother worked several jobs to make ends meet, and we came to know many babysitters. There was Charmay. She was a boy-crazy teenage girl and for the most part would spend her time flirting in the hallways with adolescent boys, flipping her hair back, and laughing out loud. My brother and I sometimes relied on bread and sugar sandwiches to fill our empty bellies, but I recall Charmay bringing her own food, proceeding to eat in front of us as we watched on like dogs begging at the dinner table, swallowing heavy with increased salivation in the mere sight of fresh vegetables. We were like Pavlov's dogs.

There was the fireman's wife; she was a plump woman with her dark hair typically thrown into a messy bun atop her head. She ran her brood of kids like the crotchety Miss Hannigan from *Little Orphan Annie*. My favorite, although I cannot recall her name, was the earthy hippy-like lady. She enjoyed taking us to the nearby woods for exciting explorations. We spent many days in a nearby creek bed wading through the water looking for arrowheads, frogs, and crawdads. She was bringing back the likeness of our time spent at the farm. I loved her long, soft brown hair, her calm personality, her delicate features, and her genuine desire to explore nature with us. She didn't last long, unfortunately, but I would never forget her. In concert with Doug's place, she gave me a profound continuation of love for all things nature.

My mother ultimately remarried. She met my stepfather, Ed, while working for the Missouri Public Interest Group as an administrative assistant. Ed stood out from the other politicians. He portrayed this rough exterior as a Korean war veteran, former fireman and coal miner. He rode a motorcycle, chain-smoked, while giving off this silent tough Clint Eastwood vibe. And according to my mother, at the time, dawned "atrocious" silk and polyester shirts and suits.

He was a city councilman. For the most part he was emotionally distant, dedicated to his work as a local politician, and like my mother an activist. They would fight a little differently but made one hell of a team. My stepfather was always at the podium with his proud wife at his side. She would help in his approach, edit his speeches, rally constituents, and later help him reach the top of the political ladder to pro-tem of the State Senate. My brother and I were often left out of that ladder. What happens to children without structure, continual parental observation, and nurturing? Demons.

FOUR

Nature Wins

I want to talk more about nature, not biology, because of the significance it had in my life. I want to discuss my coping ability, my recognition and intuition of my illness, and ultimately the grace I give myself, with the space and mindfulness that keeps me alive today. As a child growing up amidst the sinister forces taking center stage, it was the luxury of vacations that became my escape. Climbing into our family conversion van, while sitting in the bucket seat just behind my father, I stared out the window to see all my monsters standing in the front yard, like time would stand still until I returned.

Despite that, while growing up, summers were spent appealing even more to my naturalist side as we vacationed in a remote area of Orient, New York, at the very tip of Long Island, to visit my grandparents. While settled in Long Island I could count on immersing myself in the peacefulness of the sandy beach of Peconic Bay just, steps from the house, which was surrounded by a privacy fence of native shrubs and a few trees.

Waking up early meant catching the sunrise, taking deep breaths of the sea-scented air. The seagulls sang praise over their breakfast of fish and small crab. I dug my bare toes deep into the warm sand and squished them around while making my way to the shoreline, investigating all the various creatures. I tried to catch minnows with my bare hands, inspected each tiny crab and their unique shells, and skipped rocks. Occasionally, if I woke up early enough, I could catch my stepfather on his way down the beach to a quaint general store in town, where he treated me to my favorite. A fresh raspberry jelly-filled donut, which also happened to be his favorite.

When I wasn't swimming or adventuring along the beach, I biked or walked the long stretches of countryside roads, taking in the breathtaking, rich-in-history scenery. But a Greenport vacation wasn't complete without the annual backyard beachside clambake. We dug holes in the sand and filled it with seaweed and wood to create a small fire for the large seafood variety. Clams, oysters, lobster, crab, and bluefish topped with roasted corn on the cob. It was a festive bon voyage with family while filling our senses with a palatable, savory feast and robust laughter, allowing me to leave with happy memories.

Our final trek for the summers was Sault Ste. Marie, Ontario, Canada, a camplike property surrounded by dark green birch trees to a muddy bank outlining a large lake. Our vacations spent in Canada were a vastly different environment, a twenty-four-hour, around-the-clock party for both kids and adults. One single day could present anxiousness and emotional overload.

Don't get me wrong; it was a fantastic time. A kid's dream of fun in the sun. But by the time we prepared our departure I was beyond ready. By day, we went boat riding, skiing, or tubing. We went cliff diving off a small, rocky landmass in the middle of the lake, called Whiskey Island. By night, we all retreated to our age-dividing cabins. Rated G kids gone wild in one cabin with a nanny in tow.

The adults stayed in another. I can't account for the adults, but us kids watched movies, binged on food, laughed uncontrollably, barely slept, and greatly appreciated our time parentless. Not necessarily prime conditions for a child easily overstimulated, prone to environmentally induced mania. Despite the smell of the fresh air holding the distinct smell of lake water and earth or the giant trees that reach the sky and thick timber housing so much life, this was not a low-key, low-speed vacation.

Kenya

As I grew into a teenager, spring and summer commonly activated heightened impulses and an exacerbated response to environmental triggers. I committed to a flamboyant fight with my parents. An upcoming vacation fell over the weekend on which my friends would be attending the Mötley Crüe "Girls, Girls, Girls" concert without me. Reverting to toddler-like tactics, kicking and screaming from my bed in protest "I don't want to go, don't make me go!" didn't alter the course.

The vacation was a trip to Kenya for safari with my grandparents. I know what you're thinking and yes, I did in fact beg and plead to pass up the amazing opportunity to safari for live music, long hair, theatrical stage lighting, sweat, and the emotional-response hard rock music from Vince Neil and Nikki Six gave me. When you're someone who responds intensely to their environment, music can provide an outlet for emotions you otherwise can't expel. I can feel heavy beats and lyrically powerful songs deeply in my mind, body, and heart. Menacing feelings can be absorbed as a rhythm reverberates through my core. Music can be the buffer between insurmountable emotions and my response to them.

Although nature and the life that lives among it had an impact on me from an early age, it became sidelined over the years for a more destructive, unguided behavior. It wasn't at a total loss. I was aware how nature made me feel. The increased serotonin while walking the sandy beaches and the country roads of Greenpoint Long Island was irrefutable. And nature was memorable enough to have personally chosen that trip to Africa when I was at a different level on the behavioral chart.

At first sight Nairobi, Kenya is intimidating. Jomo Kenyatta Airport was rich in ethnicities, heavily guarded, and as fast-paced as JFK. A stern guard said something I didn't understand to my grandfather, who tried to defuse the situation. "Okay, okay, okay," he said while holding his hands up before him. The item causing some commotion was my luggage. A large army-green duffle bag. It appeared to have been cut open by a sharp object, then duct-taped back together. I remember wondering why they didn't just use the zipper. The silver tape was already ragged and dirty. I have no idea what my bag had been through but the look on my grandfather's face and the appearance of my bag only made me more unnerved. I later learned they may have assumed my luggage was military and wanted to double-check its contents.

I spent my first day in Nairobi confined to my hotel, puking in pain and dehydrated until the hotel physician could have a look at me. Eyeing my medication bottle, he asked me how much and how long I had been taking my anti-malaria prescription. Apparently, the label was misprinted, and I had been consuming twice the prescribed dosage for my age and weight. Not a positive start to this adventure, and I hadn't seen anything other than the city block eyed from my hotel room window.

Day two and we finally connected with a travel group. I was significantly younger than the other passengers. They immediately took note of my presence while piling into the four-wheel-drive travel van with third row seating and a pop-open roof. Their faces read: *I really hope this girl is of no trouble. Wasn't there an age requirement for this tour?* The best thing they could have done was sitting me in the front seat with our tour driver, Jonathan. The hens and their husbands held conversations about cooking tips, what they did for a living prior to retirement, their thoughts on the current political climate in certain parts of Africa, and their admiration of the view.

Just a few miles out of the city, the landscape turned to lush, kelly green fields on rolling hills. A few small, woodshed-like homes were scattered about. The colors were magnificent, a sky unfazed by the technological advances of the modern era. The ground untroubled by chemicals or the overcropped fields of corporate farming. Even on the cloudiest day with drizzling rain, the panorama from my front seat was spectacular. The cloudy, gray sky looked painted; its brush sprinkled the grass with a glistening sheen. I've never experienced anything like it before. Not in Greenport and not in Canada.

There was an abundance of wildebeests, gazelles, giraffes, and zebras for miles. The elephants represented this archaic presence, almost dignified and stoic. Their eyes said everything. They spoke of their hardships, their losses, and their unity. I found myself wanting to look them deep in the eye, and it felt like they were doing the same. They cautiously surveyed the surroundings and their young as they passed by our caravan with their own, tail to tail. At fifteen I knew nothing of poaching and the ivory trade, habitat destruction, or elephant work and performance slavery. But I felt immense sadness for the elephant that I can't explain.

The various monkeys gave off a mischievous and aloof presence. Always up to something, observing people, taking something as their own, playing about. Their skittish pranksters making for prime entertainment. Hyenas are misunderstood dark scavengers with a laugh that I think mocks a frenzied cry. I don't know why they stood out to me to even make note. Maybe their false reputation? Hyenas are actually quite loyal and are said to make friends much like we do. I can relate to this dark-sided loyal friend, unpredictable and working toward survival. We have an unorthodox kinship.

Day three we rose particularly early. The plan was to spend the day riding hot air balloons over the Serengeti. A magnificent, utterly overwhelming display, the small basket housing no more than three. My grandfather, the balloon operator, and myself. We must have been fifteen hundred feet above. High enough to be at flying level with the Silverbird's, red-capped robins, and Hildebrandt's starlings of the Serengeti. But low enough to glide across the sky just above the herds at their speed, seeing absolutely everything for fifty miles in every direction

The July weather proved perfect, forties in the mornings and around eighty by afternoon. The sun was direct but the temperature still comfortable. And in the basket, I only felt the wind in my face while consumed with the sights around me. I was brought to tears but wiped them away quickly, so no one noticed.

On day four on safari, we saw various animals in their natural habitats, villages, and tourist destinations. The children of these villages do the trading and surround our vehicle before we can even step out. My grandfather heard of this and came prepared with a box full of light-up yo-yos for bartering. He and my grandmother acquired many trinkets for their home. I picked up some beaded jewelry for friends back home and a few figurines for myself.

On day five we heard promises of a memorable trip to see a village of Masai people. The Masai are adorned in bright colors, their earlobes draping their necks, wide bands of gold stretching their necks to their limits. The young Masai male warriors performed the exuberant dance Adumu, jumping to great heights in order to prove themselves a worthy husband and warrior. Their rhythmic chants held their movements while the two warriors jumped simultaneously in the center, attempting each time to go farther than the other to establish who of them was the dominant winner. They are a proud people, also taking particular pride in herding cattle and hunting.

The village was smaller than I expected. There are approximately one million Masai in total across Africa, mostly nomads. In this village there were maybe a dozen huts formed by sticks and mud in a tightly woven structure. When we arrived, there were no Masai men, only women and children present. The men were gone, working their cattle for their livelihood. The moment I stepped inside the confines of their village, their home, I felt apprehensive. Like an intruder. How did they really feel about droves of people coming and going, gawking at them like an exhibit at the zoo? Unlike my grandparents and the rest of the party, I stood embarrassingly toward the entrance.

A single, bangle-striped kitten crossed my path and I bent down to pet it. A little Masai boy and his mother were suddenly closer to me. The Masai mother was eyeing my now dirty, oatmeal-colored Banana Republic Henley shirt. She pointed to me, then to the kitten. She must have been asking if I wanted the kitten. The little boy was now in between us, looking up at me with his forearm blocking his eyes from the sun to look at me closer. I surmised he probably wanted to know if I was going to take his kitten. The mother then grasped her dark red robe with two fingers, pinching it toward me, then pointing again to the kitten. I caught on, smiled at her, then shook my head and told her "No." As a businesswoman, she wanted to barter my shirt for the adorable feline I clearly had taken a liking to.

The little boy, in a faded patterned shirt with neutral-colored shorts, never spoke a word. Just gazed at me, watching my every move. Which wasn't much. I mostly stood awkwardly, my right hand holding my left elbow across my stomach. I fidgeted and looked back at the boy, expecting him to get bored and walk away. Only he didn't; he nor his mother left my side. Quite the opposite; she pointed me to a hut nearby. This gained the attention of my grandparents, who had no reluctance. They pushed me toward the door. "Go on in; she wants to show you."

I could not be any more uncomfortable. Even though the Masai clearly had allowed this. And I imagined the more tourists, the more money or goods to receive. I stepped inside the hut. It was dark with only the light through the door hitting the back wall. The floor was smooth dirt and there was one cot to the right. A single, torn-out magazine page of a red sports car was somehow hung to the wall. As soon as I stopped to take it in, a young Masai man appeared behind me. Unlike the mother who expressed little emotion, he was smiling with all of his white teeth. He spoke very good English, and through an accent said, "I hope to someday come to America, and in American maybe I drive that car."

It hit me all at once. I couldn't put the feeling to words then, but I know now. His smile, the normalcy of his life, the empty hut, with one bed, no items for cooking, no other blankets or clothing, and nothing more than what was on their back. Yet he smiled, enthusiastically, with no concern for the extreme minimalist lifestyle in which they lived. They knew how we lived, a lot of non-essentials, makeup, perfectly coiffed hair, clean and trendy clothes...nothing like they were accustomed to. And the young Masai man seemed not to care.

We visited the house from *Out of Africa*, stayed the night in a large-scale treehouse called the Arc built among the trees, and traveled to Mount Kilimanjaro, where I peed on the equator. I stepped in a hole of flamingo dung, then stunk up the van with my tour party for the remainder of the day. Jonathan, our driver, who was from Kenya and had experienced very little primary school but made good money for his family as a tour guide, listened to the music of Lita Ford, Bon Jovi,

Def Leppard, and Mötley Crüe through the headphones of my Walkman.

Other than being sensitive to the economic differences and the animals to which I felt emotionally connected, I wasn't having any breakdowns. Where were my monsters? I had no fits of anger, no sudden bouts of sobbing, and no manic hyperactivity. My mind was clear. Sunrises and sunsets from every travel point seemed more intense in Africa, raw against the untamed landscapes. I was in awe of the scenery and the cathartic closeness with nature I had come to love.

I wasn't meant to go to that concert, and I wasn't expected to stay home that summer with no structure or control. I was entirely where I was intended to be. Experiencing precisely what I was supposed to experience: Mother Nature's extraordinary work on the other side of the globe. I've learned some humility, increased compassion, and delight for things outside my everyday environment. A profound, unforgettable, and moving trip that someday I hoped to recreate. This trip didn't change the trajectory of my life, but it certainly was reflective of how in times of pivotal moments the universe can remind you of memories and emotions you need to hang on to.

Mother Nature

Mother Nature has the cure
To all that ails you that's for sure
Hiking, biking, climbing, and kayaking
Submit yourself to whatever your liking
From the deep green forests to the vast deep oceans
Breathe her in then let out the old
Succumb to her beauty
And you will feel peace tenfold
She enters your soul giving you grace
Enlightens you in her magical place
Mother Nature is a cure
To all that ails you that's for sure

Innocence Taken

Monsters don't always come at night
Sometimes they come by when your saviors are away
They don't discriminate age, race, or prosperity
Lurking in their wicked ways judging vulnerability
Testing all the corners like a shark
Praying on the innocent from dark shallows
Attacks so cunning you question your validity
Scars so deep you feel their ridges without exception
Many can't see what you can feel
Even finding skepticism in your ordeal
Like the walking stick hiding in plain sight
Moving in aimless contradictory
Monsters permanently change a victim's trajectory
Now they long for the life they may never see
Innocence taken without permission
A silent killer by definition—that needs more verbal recognition

FIVE

Environmental Sinister Forces

Despite his absence in my youth, my stepfather left an impact on my life that is almost indescribable. Within my undiagnosed mental illness, I was waging war to make his life miserable through childhood and teenage angst. Life became a little more complicated. My mind was occasionally despondent, morose, and forlorn. Other times it was disconnected and quiet, with feelings of confusion and paranoia. I wouldn't find comfort in the seclusion of my mind, nor nature, nor music. I would come to know my darkness in varying forms. It crept in over time; it was elusive yet relentless when it presented itself.

I had very few friends minus my neighbors Emily and Joseph, who lived behind me in an old two-story house. Their mother was a highly intelligent marathon runner. Emily most certainly obtained the gift of intelligence from her; she was by all accounts in my young mind a genius. Emily was in all the advanced classes, always focused on school and grades. Everything I wasn't. Interestingly enough, much like my high school best friend, Lisa. She too was committed to her education, while I was anything but. Seems ironic I would become so close to two very together friends. Differences aside, Emily and I had a great connection over music and mixtapes, sunning ourselves in her backyard, and long walks around the neighborhood holding the giddiest of girl talks.

Regardless of my growing disdain for boys, I often hung out with the siblings two doors to our east: John, Jeff, and Jason. They lived with their father, who was a reticent, polite man who reminded me of a Mennonite in appearance. Small beard and suspenders over a collared shirt. They say one in four girls experiences sexual abuse in their lifetime, yet even with those alarming statistics my neighbors John, Jeff, and Jason remained different. The boys seemed to have been taught an enormous amount of respect from their father. They were the only childhood male friends I had who weren't trying to grope me in some way. The boys and I often spent hours in a nearby creek bed as explorers. Play flag football, walk the neighborhood, or hang out to watch episodes of their favorite cartoon, *Speed Racer*.

Given the archaic patriarchy, even young girls are subject to sexual harassment and abuse by their peers in the classroom. Deeply embedded, underlying teachings that women and girls are only here to satisfy the sexual urges of men create women who grow to believe this is their value, then who raise daughters to believe it too. As a culture we don't stand in the way of the sexualization of girls by social media, advertisements, television, and movies. Our boys are brainwashed immediately to see this as the adequate and normal interpretation to view girls and women.

Other boys I knew tried to convince me they needed a wrestling partner but only wanted to rub themselves on me from behind or swipe their arms across my prematurely developed breasts. One neighbor boy four years my senior tried to convince me he had feelings for me in a way I wasn't mature enough to even comprehend. He would run his fingers down my arm so that his knuckles would drag the edges of my breasts and nipples. There were the boys in my fifth-grade classroom who would blatantly run into me pretending to throw their hands up to stop themselves and cop a feel. Or the boys in my gym class who would point, stare, and snicker as I did jumping jacks to see my newly young breasts bounce just enough to their delight. But the most impactful was the male family member who abused me in a far sinister way.

These experiences set a path for me as a hormonal, mentally ill young girl. I was for obvious reasons swimming in a pool of self-hatred while floating on a wave of insecurities. Add to that cocktail abandonment issues and in almost textbook fashion I sabotaged my life immensely in every way imaginable. To the delight of my darkness, I would go on to dabble in drug use and experienced alarming hypersexuality in my waves of mania. The difficulty for me, a sexual abuse survivor, is the desperate desire to have respect for my own body after having given so much of it away during manic states.

Growing into the presence of all my distractions I attempted navigating through high school as an extremely timid, lost, and untrusting young woman. Fall and winter drain my body of serotonin, leaving little for reserve. This allows my mind to open freely to the darkness my monster manifests while skillfully manipulating me. This hijacker wastes no time in his seasonally based overhaul. Scared, worthless, unattractive, and despairing. This disposition requires physical alterations to drive home the self-destructive broken and bad girl theme. Dark clothes, carefully black-lined eyes, my shoulder-length tresses shaved to the scalp in Brittany-esque fashion. Leaving nothing more than some short '80s version of a mullet.

Spring and summer lunacy looked vastly different. Like a wolf rising in the night from human form to howl at the moon. The alluring, even seductive, Luna, leading my monster and me in a parallel circadian rhythm to hers. Pouring from my frontal lobe confidence, engaging charm, and humor. I know no boundaries; nothing is off-limits. I am drawn to follow every whim with extraordinary exuberance. My teenage body perfectly balances testosterone and estrogen, initiating lust, while dopamine and norepinephrine drive hypersexual attraction. Everything feels good. You don't need ecstasy when you have bipolar mania.

Hair is grown and loose, subtle makeup, highlighting my summer tan. Significant weight loss at any means necessary so my clothes are flattering and fitted to my small frame. I carry an arsenal of verbiage to acquire cash from my parents to fund my impulsive and reckless undertaking. Maybe sneak out to meet Mike the Marine, seven years my senior, for parties, drinks, and sex. Daytime drives in his Jeep with the sun on our faces, high and free in endless laughter. Or maybe I'll partake in hours-long motorcycle rides with tan and buff Bill. We were the only two people on earth. Untethered to the world, doing whatever I wanted, when I wanted. More drinking, more sex, and more parties. But mania doesn't come without great ramifications.

SIX

Ramifications

I can still smell the sterile hospital hallways as I recount that day. A young resident doctor came to perform my first sonogram. I was seventeen and excited to learn the sex of my baby despite the circumstances. The resident, calm and quiet, never skipped a beat, announcing she had to step out and seek assistance as she was struggling with the equipment. A matronly senior physician presented herself, picked up the sonogram probe, and ran it across my abdomen for several minutes, quiet with a hint of concern on her face.

I sensed pretty quickly that something wasn't right. Wiping the jelly from my stomach, she asked me to sit up so we could discuss her findings. This part is mostly a blur. In the most unvarnished, sobering manner she said, "I am unable to detect a fetal heartbeat." Her words faded in and out as I tried to wrap my mind around exactly what that meant. She continued, they could either induce labor to deliver immediately or send me home until my body would "reject the fetus." It was all so fast. There was no empathetic show of patience to process, let alone make medical decisions for myself under such duress. Confused, shattered, and with no one at my side, I opted to stay and induce labor.

Placed in a cold and impersonal semi-private room, I felt isolated behind the pale blue dividing curtain. Very few staff came to check on me, and the halls seemed particularly empty. It's as if I was intentionally placed at the far end of the corridor to ensure I didn't interfere with the happiness of mothers delivering full-term babies. Or maybe it was to protect me from them. Slowly my body began to work accordingly with the Pitocin, forcing this baby from me. I wasn't ready. I didn't get to process the pain, the loss, or even understand why this was happening.

There was no nurse or doctor at my side to guide me or console me. My father had arrived in time to abruptly seek support, calling frantically down the hallway when my twenty-week, eleven-ounce baby descended from my body, ending lifeless between my legs. The stiff umbilical cord was still attached, gray in appearance; the tiny head was substantial to its body. Everything went quiet; my father's voice in the hall was indistinct. And for a minute, we were the only two in this still room.

The nurse arrived without making eye contact. She didn't ask me about my pain scale from one to ten, say she was sorry for my loss, or talk to me about what symptoms I might feel post-delivery. She only swooped my baby up within a stack of white towels that lay nearby and proceeded to place its meager body into a bucket. A moment forever etched into my memory as clear as recalling the sky is blue. It's as if the nurse was taking out the trash, my lifeless infant placed in a white five-gallon pail, when she suddenly seemed to recall some ounce of moral decency, or simply remembered a step in her training on compassion. She looked at me with little emotion to say, "Oh, did you want to hold it first?" Further devastated, I could only muster up enough courage to faintly and breathlessly ask, "Is it a boy or a girl?"

The universe placed a grief counselor there the next morning. She handed me a pamphlet about grief groups and the journey of loss. I answered some of her questions regarding if I had seen or held my baby, and if I knew what my options were with burial or cremation. Not only had I not received this information, but I also had no idea of their existence, or that I would even be here experiencing this. Just twenty-four hours prior I was unsuspectingly walking in to find if I would be bringing home a Jacob Ryan or Hannah Rose in twelve weeks. I took all the information she provided, attended a grief meeting or two, and requested a funeral. It was exactly the closure I needed.

My mother convinced a rabbi and friend to perform a funeral service despite Jewish laws about this. When a baby is not full-term, it's not common Jewish practice to have a funeral arranged. A few days later, my son, Jacob Ryan, was laid to rest in a picturesque part of a cemetery near a pond referred to at the front gate as the Home for Little Angels. Maybe Jacob and I weren't meant to be. Had I gone full-term, maybe I would never have had my subsequent children in the order that I did. He wasn't meant to be mine, and I wasn't meant to be his. I lovingly envision his little face having been born to someone else, joyful and giggling.

My Little Angel

I can't keep you
You are not mine
God has other plans
It's straight from the divine
Mommy loves you to the moon
I am sorry you had to go so soon
You'll be somewhere safe
Joyfully embraced
Good luck my little dear
Your fate is clear
Someday I'll see you again
When my soul is ready to ascend
Your time here is done
So be brave little one
A new life for you has just begun

Exes

I have a few exes
The alcoholic
The self-righteous
The overly obnoxious
No one will seal my fate
But each painted me with a blood red mark
So deep it bleeds from every "please" and "stop"
From the "I don't care" to the "don't you dare"
I have a few exes
Each painted a blood red mark
So deep I feel week
From the topsy-turvy of this roller coaster derby
From a life each one brought

SEVEN

Of Men & Monsters, Husband I

A drunk-fueled, violent, and chaotic relationship describes my first marriage to Mike the Marine. We ignited this chaotic storm of madness that was defined by grand highs and lows, from domestic assaults to untapped adoration in a Sid and Nancy Vicious kind of way. Volatile as our two bipolar brains, never in sync, we clashed in every way possible. Never on the same manic wave. Neither of us was aware of our illness, but we both knew our monsters and we spoke of them.

Mike was eight years older, looked fine in a Marine uniform, undoubtedly intelligent, voted best looking of his high school graduating class, and had been captain of the football team. I had this dreamlike claim of a life with him. We indulged in jazz and blues festivals, observed nature boots on the ground. Mike was an amazing cook, taking pride in all his creations. My parents adopted his chili recipe as the official Christmas Eve dinner. A side of white rice, shredded cheese, and chopped onions for garnish. Sober, Mike was charismatic. His smile and conversational wit won people over.

I had my first son shortly after I buried Jacob. Mike wasn't his father; he was the result of manic exploit with another man. But that didn't matter. He was my first love, although he always deserved better. After moving in with Mike the violence crept in. Starting with drunken rages and unwarranted jealousy. Not to mention, I was raised by a Jewish New Yorker. Keeping quiet was never my strong suit. My mouth and temper certainly didn't lend to peaceful negotiations.

When Mike drank, he was mouthy, spoke down to me, and spewed verbal abuse about my shortcomings. I recall vividly arriving home to our apartment from work after he had been home drinking all day. I must have been slow to arrive. Maybe I got gas; maybe I was just driving slowly. I don't recall. "Where the fuck have you been?" he slurred to me. "What are you talking about? I have been at work," I said. "Don't fucking talk back to me, you stupid bitch." Something about his words, "you stupid bitch," filled me with anger.

There was a large Styrofoam cup on the kitchen counter. With little thought of repercussions, I filled it with water, walked within a short distance of him seated on the sofa, and tossed all thirty-two ounces of fluid toward his face. "Why don't you just fucking cool off." Probably not the wisest decision, as it took mere milliseconds for Mike to jump from the sofa to my throat. He wasn't making any sense.

"You think just because you work, you're better than me?" With one hand choking my neck he took a beer in his other hand and doused it all over me. "How does that feel, you fucking bitch? You don't deserve this shirt you're wearing. I paid for this."

Freeing his hand from the beer can, he began tearing my button-down blouse from me. I pulled and screamed, "Mike, stop, stop, please stop." His ranting became so belligerent I somehow freed myself from his grip and ran down the hallway trying to get to the bedroom before he did. Did I think he couldn't get me through that flimsy, cheap, hollow door? Mike met me in the room to again remind me I was nothing compared to him. He ripped the remainder of the wet shirt from my body and then smothered my face with it. I couldn't scream or breathe.

He took the shirt from my face long enough for me to catch a breath. Exhaustion was setting in, but adrenaline kept me fighting. Grabbing my hair, he once again muffled my cries by pushing my face into the nearby mattress. I was trying to kick, use my arms as leverage, anything to obtain my natural instinct to breathe. Taunting me, he lifted me up by my hair. His strength seemed to come from nowhere and I was no match. I was tired. I wanted it to end. My muscles hurt, my throat hurt, and my head where he pulled me by my hair hurt. I was not screaming anymore. Only cries; muffled, faint cries. Mike put his hand all the way around my neck, and with shear anger driving his tirade, took his other hand to my thigh and lifted me off the ground. His hand to my neck felt like a noose. He threw me like a ragdoll across the room, then looked at me in a "see, this is what you get" look, as he walked out.

This was one of many episodes. A bat to the face, a cylinder block to the cheek, neighbors shielding me behind their doors as he looked for me. And a gut-wrenching plea for aid from the apartment manager. "We just want to know you're okay. Your neighbors and I are concerned. Please let me know if I can help you in any way." We moved many times, trying a new fresh start, a new rehab program, new jobs, but nothing was a match for our monsters.

I visited Mike in rehab once only to share in one manic moment. We both crept off to a bathroom for a quickie. It was like old times: the Jeep, the woods, the festivals spent dancing, food, and music. The moments weren't ever enough. We had two beautiful children. One girl and then one boy. Who by all accounts deserved far greater than we ever gave them. I stayed. I felt I was supposed to carry out the "in sickness and in health" vow. That his alcoholism was an excuse, a disease. But as my motherly instincts to protect my young increased so did his violence. When I was seeking spiritual solace in Buddhism, he was far removed from God or any spiritual inkling. A few separations and ten years would be the limit.

Mike never regained sobriety. Spent some time in prison for violating an ex-part I filed, evicted from several homes, and eventually on the streets homeless. Many years later, Mike was found unconscious on a motel floor. His body detoxed while he lay unconscious for approximately three days. Detoxing at his level of alcoholism without medical intervention caused a crash in B1. The result of this was Wernicke-Korsakoff syndrome. Otherwise known as "wet brain." A devastating and permanent brain damage, particularly involved in memory. He now lives his life in a nursing home. He has little to no family or friends. Our children either won't or find it difficult to see him in his condition. And Mike is only left able to recite episodes of his glory days in high school football and the Marine Corp before his downfall.

EIGHT

Of Monsters & Men, Husband II

It's not hard to learn that physical pain heals much faster than mental. There is no pill, and sometimes it seems there's not enough therapy to heal from the scars branded into your brain. The cuts of verbal and emotional torment come with searing pain while casting a web of confusion to which you aren't even sure of who you are anymore. The psychopaths capable of this behavior do it unapologetically. My second husband was such a creature. He consciously makes an effort to deceive his victims for a self-centered result, without empathy or emotional attachment.

Being blindsided is one of the worst offenses you can experience. My first husband never tried to hide who he was. Not the alcoholism, not the volatility. Even in the unpredictability, he was predictable. He never tried to set a mental or physical image of another character to ensure his odds. But my second husband did just that. *He falsified a positive persona that he never intended to maintain.* He had a goal, entice then propose in a clear conquest in portraying an exterior materialistic family. The good jobs, the nice house, the kids in all the latest trends, and all that the modern-day joneses would have. It's when you don't live up to these stringent expectations that his victims lay stunned and cast to the wayside.

Naturally, on a spring manic high, I fell for the charm and in a few short weeks he proposed. He begged me to consider more children since he didn't have an heir to his name. I found it hard to resist the high on the vitamin D my skin was soaking up in my spring and summer mania. Hyper-sexual, up for anything, feeling impulsive, and ready to go. My monster gallantly guided the surfboard toward the sun and mayhem. I became pregnant with my fourth child, was substitute teaching, and doing my best to make ends meet financially. In the eyes of the psychopath, I wasn't living up to my end of the bargain. "You're a deadbeat mother" was just one of his go-to assaults. Add in the young woman who contacted me to fill me in on their exploits together.

I felt sickened, physically nauseous, fearful, and uncertain. I faced the possibility of raising four kids alone with little to no income. He made me feel like he was the victim, that I was the aggressor in my tirade for answers. He barely spoke to me, left, then came back, and ceased all intimacy. Of course, sex wasn't off the table if it suited him. I was an incubator. A vessel to deliver his baby. Nothing more. Yet I did nothing. Frozen in emotional fear, weak, a pitiful representation of a mother with her children's best interest at heart.

I certainly wasn't the only one suffering his Dr. Jekyll/Mr. Hyde transition. He failed to give positive attention to the children and punished them for trivial behaviors. Lack of positive attention or fatherly shared moments. Our house was his prison, and he, the warden. There isn't a cap on the self-castigation one mother can conduct on herself to bring back the years. Crushing, inexcusable, life-altering moments punch shame into your gut with such veracity the pain will never subside. Exactly as it shouldn't. They manifest through my oldest son, already emotional and broken, looking to me with tears streaking his face. "If this is what it is to have a dad, I don't ever want one." I deserve every scar those words come with. I carry that burden willingly without argument.

Everyone else felt the storm too. When I agreed to marry this man, the last-minute conjectures weren't silenced. My stomach tried to hold it together with waves of nerves and fear while I sat in contemplation. In the mirror I looked beautiful; my bundle bump looked beautiful too. My hair was perfectly placed in a classic updo, thoughtfully done by my best friend. My mother and father were anxious yet stoically at my side. "You don't have to go through with this…. I can walk out this door and ask all the guests to leave." Mother knows best. Why didn't I listen? Why didn't she press harder? Why couldn't I do what I knew was right? Why did I do it?

Why did I spend hours crying on the floor of my bathroom when he left again? Why did I beg him to "do the right thing" by us? I didn't even want him. Not truly. My conscious mind was full of degrading vulnerabilities while my subconscious, my light, my pillar of courage, could only coach from the sidelines. Watching as I fought against every play in the playbook of joy and success with disturbing ease.

I can't articulate how I ended up in this situation, with this man, other than for some reason the universe wanted me to have my youngest daughter. On slim odds, my daughter was born on the same day around the same time as my first son was born deceased those years back. I don't question the force behind nature's inviolable interventions. She wasn't given to me; I was selected. Honored to be bestowed with the heart and soul of not only my youngest daughter but all of my children. I never felt worthy of their youthful adoration. And to this day, I try to live to their magnificence.

Again, And Again

Self-hatred so deep with each cut
I've punched my own face fearing nothing will heal this
    fucking rut
Every nerve in my body like pins in my gut
I let the water run over my face to silence this shitty luck
Again, and again, a voice creeps into my ear
It reminds me not to fear
That monster who tries to hold me so near
So, I awaken from this crazed state
To begin another day, a new blank slate

NINE

Of Monsters & Men, Husband III

"A true soul mate is probably the most important person you'll ever meet because they tear down your walls and smack you awake. But to live with a soul mate forever? Nah. Too painful. Soul mates, come into your life just to reveal another layer of yourself to you and then leave.

"A soul mate's purpose is to shake you up, tear apart your ego a little bit, show you your obstacles and addictions, break your heart open so new light can get in, make you so desperate and out of control that you have to transform your life, then introduce you to your spiritual master..."

—Elizabeth Gilbert, *Eat, Pray, Love*

There have never been such truer words. It takes this person, your soul mate, to truly withstand the abundantly colossal movements of your emotional existence. My soul mate had the shoulders of a giant, the skin of a rhinoceros, the temperament to disconnect, the humor to keep life light, and the heart to be clement and magnanimous. Throughout our tempestuous marriage, I accused my soul mate of being selfish, unthoughtful, and cold. Little did I know, he was so much more than my accusations.

My third husband came to me right when I needed that stable, humorous, gentle presence. The bonus was the consistency and predictability he added to the lives of my children. Turbulence is never far behind me, however. My moods unpredictable, my mania increasingly alarming with inescapable consequences. The perfect set of circumstances and conditions cooperatively in sync with hysteria shadows my every move. Unresolved past relationship traumas add to out-of-character conduct. The first, an affair within the first two years of our marriage. The most unforgivable of all marital sins.

Forgiveness is a fickle trait. It's so easy to forgive those who hurt us, but not to forgive ourselves. My third husband invariably forgave me. Undeservingly and selflessly, he set aside his pain and confusion to extend loyal, deep-seated love. Something I lacked. Yet he would forgive me again and again. Similar to my first husband, we consumed copious amounts of alcohol, partied often, and fought as if it were a set of rules we needed to check. Alcohol, check. Party, check. Fight, check. Outside of that, we laughed bounteously. We used humor as a buffer, a sealant to the cracks, a cooling agent to the heated instability. This I loved.

Mania for me is like this earthly pull through a window with one frame, intense in every regard, thought, vision, and drive. All wrapped in exaggerated perceptions. The most outrageous of tasks seems attainable. Seeing a movie about soldiers can manifest into an impulsive trip to the recruiters, convinced this is the best thing you need to feel free, to overcome weakness. I did just that. In June 2008 at age thirty-four, I enlisted in the Army Reserves. And with little regard to my family, by September I was turning thirty-five in basic training.

Even in marital discord, and that's being subtle, he still found it in his heart to be the supporting husband. My father came to our home shaken with fear over my unforeseen move. "I used to think at least you were a good mother. Now I don't even think that." He took his plea to my husband: "You don't understand, she fails at everything she does." My third husband confirmed his resolve for me, standing up to my father. No one has ever expressed such belief in me. Not in the history of my existence. I shit on his devotedness, and the consequences to my family were great.

In a small window, some dust settles. Desperately trying to make sense of this time. Who am I? What is wrong with me? I hold on to a prayer for moral strength out of a Jewish prayer book. I focus on my body, my mind, and my spirituality. I grasp for anything, an ounce of familiarity of the suppressed me. I desperately want to come to life again, remove the fog and the monsters. When clarity presents, I focus on forgiveness, making amends. My husband, the dutiful spouse, never rejects me.

My third husband's character allows me the freedom to toggle in and out of church, temple, therapy, exercise, music, medications, and simply being family-focused to redemption. I hold on to this time dearly, not knowing when I will be gone again. Mundane is an improvement, though the splinters of past mistakes still ache and hold me accountable and test my husband's motivation to stay. Why should he? Why does he? Our verbal assaults back and forth plague over any good moments.

> *Fresh starts are about the burden for the void in our hearts.*
> *You can take away the sight and unravel it in delight.*
> *Nothing feels more temporarily free than entirely new scenery.*
> *How long will it last, before you're saddled with the past once more?*

Fresh Start I

Our new brick home settled on its acre plot. It was surrounded by many more acres lined with thin layers of bush and timber and filled with crops. It radiated a tranquility reminiscent of Doug's farm. The sun rose refreshingly calm while I sipped coffee off the back porch each morning. Nestled in the backyard were a water well, an old-fashioned clothesline, a propane tank, and a small red and white shed shaded by an aged oak tree.

Breezes came in off the fields toward the house, sweeping across my face. I closed my eyes, took it in with deep breaths, and focused on nothing but the musical sounds of birds singing, the wind swaying the tree branches back and forth, and the leaves in a subtle rhythm and harmony to the crickets and frogs chipping as backup.

We arrived on July 4th weekend while the small-town festivities were in full swing. A carnival was underway at the town square surrounded by an old-fashioned pharmacy, VFW hall, local bank, and one family-owned restaurant. Newly arriving food trucks, rides, local produce, craft booths, small business owners, and local fire and police with their vehicles lined the streets. The agenda was packed and prompt: Little Mr. & Mrs. pageant first, then a newlywed game transpired, bringing laughs as local couples were put on the spot for entertainment. Followed by a full band lineup.

I readily indulged in the usual suspects of cotton candy and funnel cake. My third husband followed along, aloof. My youngest daughter was lured to the Ferris wheel. The riders' hands in the air, feet dangling, with robust laughter heard in each downdraft of each rotation. I was in utter delight with my new surroundings and comforts of this cozy little town. I looked forward to being a part of its appeal, feeling free from the usual distractions.

Fresh Start II

My third husband was hard to let go of. I both loved him and resented his presence. He brought me laughter, tears, pain, and bouts of happiness. The weight of my emotions for him were sizable. Once a divine intervention, aligning just right, security, peace from the chaos, and calmness from a storm. He was often the victim in this scenario. He served a significant purpose, and his task was great. A therapist once used an analogy to describe us: "Have you heard the story of the tortoise and the hare? See, you are the tortoise…" She pointed her pen toward my husband. "…and your wife is the hare." My second husband deadened me from the inside out, leaving this now engrained defense mechanism rearing its ugly head in my third marriage disconnecting in times of emotional stress. Avoidance was common, primarily because my experience with derealization adopted the defense of indifference. Completely apathetic.

A walking cautionary tale. I also wanted and needed physical and emotional validation at a heightened level. I wanted to be kissed, a desire for him to acknowledge if I looked pretty. I needed to hear the words "I love you." This kept us tangled in a continuum of unproductive debates and arguments. My husband wanted to remain intentionally unaware of my demons, dismissive of my cyclic destructive behavior or triggers. Still caught in the trap of our past. My heinous immoral escapades. My third husband was not suited to handle one more manic episode. The consistent upheaval was just so damaging for everyone. His relationship was now strained with our children; what I was doing, what I had done, was not fair. Loyal to the very end, I would have to set him free. Disconnect and make the move.

Me: "I'm sorry, I think I am moving out."

Him: "Are you serious?"

Fuck this hardened heart

This hardened heart hurts my chest
It aches and aches with no rest
Although it claims to be without feeling
It weeps and screams for the lack of love it's receiving
It blocks the affections from all who profess it without
    hesitation
Because everyone knows it's all fake
Entangled in lies and miscommunication
Fuck this hardened heart
Its burden is tearing me apart
Although it keeps me from being weak
My life will remain bleak
I miss the simple caress of all the loving emotions hugging
    my breast
Squeezing from my heart all that protests
Fuck this hardened heart
Just give me yet another fresh start

TEN

Addiction

Addiction comes in many perceptions by society. It's the ones you can see that are acknowledged. Much like how medical diagnoses are accepted but mental diagnoses don't get the same merit. A drug addict, thin, pale, sunken-in features, sores on their face, and flailing about in uncoordinated movements while talking to the air. That is more acknowledged. Even an anorexic, frail, skeletally thin, brittle hair, dark circles under the eyes, and overly pronounced cheekbones in relation to their small frame is given some value.

Those are the images of societally accepted addictions. But those of average or large frame claiming addiction under the guise of binge eating or even bulimia? That is not a comprehensible excuse. It's a weakness treated with the verbal prescription of "just stop." Just as drug addicts and anorexics, bingers come to their current fate after years of environmental contributors and a pinch of genetic predisposition.

I have an invisible illness with an invisible addiction that both comes and goes in waves of severity and depth. I acknowledge their existence and that is enough for me. The addiction to food is far more personal. My mental illness is an assault from my brain directed at me. But food is the assault I direct on myself for feelings of deep inadequacies, self-loathing, and the inability to manifest emotions appropriately. It is a self-taught subconscious war and defense mechanism all at the same time. It's so ingrained that the fight or flight to food seems to happen in muscle memory alone.

Do I do it as a result of sexual abuse and the constant sexualization by boys and men? Was it my subconscious way to make myself unattractive in order to avoid further victimization? Is it a genetic predisposition? Or was it the barrage of criticism from my mother manifesting in the hyper-focus on food? A self-fulfilling prophecy of failure, so to speak. Was it the aligned positive memories creating emotional soothing during events around a meal? I acknowledge that food, and its savory flavors, can incite feelings of relief, comfort, and joy in situations of stress, sadness, and even celebration. And is it now in fact a muscle memory so beyond conscious recognition it's out of my control? The answer is yes to all of the above.

Saying my addiction to food feels like muscle memory more than cognizant thought isn't far off. Eating food for all the reasons I identified creates a flood of dopamine in my pleasure center. Then the development of tolerance and compulsion takes over. The pleasure ultimately subsides, and normal motivation is no longer the driving force. Embedded memories help create a conditioned response and cravings whenever I encounter specific environmental cues. This is often the relapse after sobriety. It's the reason that even in times of contentment I am still not in the driver's seat.

The contributing factors were still always the groundwork for the eating disorder, but the mental illness escalated my emotional response. In a moment of heightened sensitivity, I was significantly harder on myself. My monsters altered the way in which I viewed even my physical self. My face rounder, my nose flatter, my eyes puffy and dark. My hair was uncooperative, the color was not right, the texture coarse and unmanageable. A single hair or section commandeered the intensified hysteria. Depending on my cabinet's arsenal, hair dye was frantically applied, or scissors madly chopped at all the out-of-control places. The dust settled almost always in regret and an embarrassing visit to the hairdresser.

Although in times of mania, anorexia seemed almost effortless. Weight fell off quickly and my confidence rose. But in times of depression, I couldn't understand why my mouth and body behaved unreasonably. When attempts to not eat failed me, one, two, three, no four laxatives should do it. Staring at myself in the mirror, tears streamed freely. A pure rage built quite rapidly and required a target. "Why are you so disgusting?" "You make me sick." "I fucking hate you." This became an internal dialogue I grew accustomed to.

The verbal attack didn't satisfy the rage. I needed pain. Pain to release some of the rageful energy built up in my face, my fists, my chest. "I fucking hate you" guided my own open hand to strike my face, and then with my fist. I punched my face in unison to the verbal abuse. "You're fat and disgusting." I cried, "Look at you—you're nothing." The diatribe and physical blows drained me in one instance. My roaring bellows shifted to subdued sobs as I slumped to my bathroom tile floor. I was defeated, crippled, and resigned to my repulsion.

Scenes like that repeat over the discomfort of clothing, an unpleasant conversation, unwavering feelings of sadness, the awakening after a manic episode, and really anything that makes me feel substandard. A violent display born from unrealistic expectations that my mind manifested over time. I'm forty-six now, and the battle between my body and the magnet called food still impacts my overall self-worth. Not quite to the violent displays of before, but the nagging of disappointment, the fear of public scrutiny.

The addiction and the habitual yo-yo of control and powerlessness affect so much more than just physical appearance and the way in which I torture myself. It affects every facet of my life, such as how I parent two daughters, and my sons for that matter, as they determine their own self-worth. I think about how each of them regularly engages in diets, exercise, or supplements to maintain a mental expectation they have created for themselves.

It affects my socialization and friendships when I make excuses to not meet for events or gatherings. I'm likely hiding from embarrassment due to an exaggerated muffin top, an uncomfortable bra, the way my arms look in the quarter sleeves, or how my thighs don't come together with my calves as an hourglass meeting at my knees. My brother once said my legs were like drumsticks.

The effect that impacts me more at this age is the one to my marriage. A despise for my body coupled with sexual trauma is a disaster to the intimacy and sexual relationship of a marriage. My husband genuinely loves me and every inch of my curves and tells me so almost daily. If he isn't saying it, he shows it. Showing brings its own dilemma. When he wants to hug me, he isn't thinking about where to place his hands. He's not thinking, *I'll place my hands squarely on her hips as to not touch her belly fat*. No, he goes all in. Hands ending up wherever they may.

I shudder. My skin literally crawls to the touch as I snap with a sharp "Don't...stop touching my fat" as I squirm, loosening his grip from whatever part of my body unworthy of his love. I have forced myself to allow him to hug me from behind while I work on something in the kitchen. His arms are completely and tightly around me. He is taking me all in with his adoration. If he could see my face, he would be confused, maybe even internalize my emotions as if there is something wrong with him.

I find myself so significantly uncomfortable, disgusted actually, that I'm desperately holding back tears. My body is stiffened, and I beg for it to be over. I'm in a defensive response to his touch and even feel anger rising. Our sexual intimacy can be obsolete. I feel every extra curve, roll, lump, and dent of cellulite as I lay in bed, and the last thing I want is to illuminate all of that with light and nakedness.

Food isn't my only weakness. If I am not careful, I have a predisposition to alcohol as well. I'm lured by the soothing properties of a lack of inhibition, making serious daily undertones light and tolerable. The ease of pouring a glass of wine, stopping for a drink with a friend, picking up something cheap from the gas station to relax after an exasperating day. It's fast-acting with irrefutable success. But of course, as we all know, its ability to temporarily diminish demons can come with significant repercussions.

The DUI, an embarrassing experience, was one significant low point. I left the bar after celebrating my birthday, repeatedly telling a friend, "No, I am fine, I'm fine." I subsequently left that parking lot and drove my truck over the grass-filled curb dividing the parking spots and main road. I managed the highway until my purse dropped into the passenger seat and I swerved to retrieve it. This induced immediate suspicion to the parked police officer watching a truck at two o'clock in the morning swerve between lanes on the highway.

Being pulled over, I quietly and politely acquiesced to every command. "Ma'am, can you walk one foot in front of the other with your arms stretched out beside you?" Obliging his request, I began my semi-stable catwalk, then stopped. "Ma'am, what are you doing?"

"Sir, I am rolling up my pants so I can see my feet better." That should help, right? Followed by, "These are my new boots—aren't they cute?"

"Ma'am, can you get seated in the front of my patrol car?"

This truly pleasant police officer after laughing at my sheer candid excitement over new shoes attempted to help me by asking repeatedly if there was anyone, he could contact for me. With a dead cellphone, and refusing to call my parents out of embarrassment, I offered up no one. He then did the only thing he could do. He Mirandized me, cuffed me, and took me to the drunk tank. Honestly, it's what I deserved.

I may have deserved the night in jail, but my youngest son didn't deserve a mother who was unable to attend his peewee football game. I can overcome the fees, the hours of community service, and the criminal record, but I can't get back the memories lost. As my first husband received the most severe of consequences, so did his children.

They're left with the memories of his inconsistent presence and the feelings of abandonment. His unstable environment and fear of his erratic behavior. They must accept their scars with any hopes of closure to be as lost as his mind.

The Binger

For the binger
For the purger
For every emotional indulger
You can hide a lot in a pound of fat
Your sadness
Your gladness
And your madness
You stuff them deep inside
Only to feel them thighs
But you keep eating anyway
Despite how sick you feel
The rolls, the lumps, from every meal
You despise every inch
But you can't stop not for a flinch
You can hide a lot in a pound of fat
Even though it will only set you back

ELEVEN

Everybody Loves a Manic Girl

Mania is a multifaceted and unpredictable result of bipolar disorder. A timeline offers a genuine look at the biologically deep response to my unique experience with mania. The acknowledgment of a defined cyclic chart of behavior shows a lack of control. It shows the hard-wired movements of my brain bound to a biological clock. One in which I have no authority.

Stages to its presence produce vastly different consequences. For me, each initial phase is a side capable of putting to action anything I can or want to accomplish. Storms of energy guided by my tenacious drive to do things for the greater good of humanity. Drives that lack boundaries, structure, and the forethought of long-term goals or necessities.

Drives to enroll in college for a degree in psychology to help those like me. Environmental sciences to save the planet. Marketing, appealing to my creative side. Law after a community college professor suggested I pursue it. Political science to follow in my father's footsteps as a senator. Become a nature photographer. A nutrition coach, to which I have three certifications. Obtain a communications degree, to be the next best war reporter. Heck, just join the Army. Or write a book!

All of which I actively pursued at one point or another. After a project has begun, it starts to lose momentum and luster. The darker forces vying for my attention begin to intrude. The reasons for my introductory grandiose impulses become forgotten. My high goes from innocent to unpredictable and erratic, leaving an overwhelming sense of dissatisfaction and unsettled. I chase the initial high through paranoia, agitation, and rage.

From an outside perspective this can look insidiously different than my convoluted perception. It's starting a project, then withdrawing in the realization I was in over my head after taking it on like an insane scientist. It's watching a movie about war and enlisting in the Army at age thirty-five, leaving behind my children. It's being the life of the party, to excessive drinker, to DUI, affairs, and sexually assaulted. It's confusing friends and family with my temporary outgoing personality to be withdrawn and quiet and then back again. It's snapping over miniscule irritants and a hypersensitivity to every noise, voice, and movement around me. And so much more.

To my children it's seeing me cater to their every whim. Last-minute trips or events. Shopping sprees with money no object. Lots of laughter and increased nurturing. Then hostile and disconnected. Like telling my oldest daughter I would be separating from my third husband while she played on the floor with her dolls. As if I was informing her of something insignificant. Even as she cried, I had no emotional response. To my mother and father, it was seeing a glimmer of hope in my upbeat boost of motivation while still wondering when the next dramatic upheaval would take place.

Mania is whiplash of feeling extraordinary then unhinged over and over again. Some experiences display this transition of madness perfectly. Such as my affair with a man we will call as I knew him in rank, Staff Sargent (SSG). People of authority, particularly men, hold not only a level of respect but that of being capable, together, particularly in chaos. Someone like this can validate my ego, make me feel valued and worthy. More importantly, safe, offering a shield from my unpredictable darkness.

I took notice of SSG not long after I arrived at his unit. It was winter, when I am typically weak and withdrawn. I actively observed his demeanor, his overall presence, and how those around me responded to him. SSG commandeered respect from every soldier in our unit. Not only by his experience as a soldier himself, but his need to ensure the success of every soldier under him. Then spring approached, along with the sun and vitamin D-induced mania. Every new relationship began with intense adoration, undivided attention, lack of sexual boundaries, humor, and the all-in tenacity of a newlywed couple. And this one would be no different.

I was required to maintain a current physical fitness test, to which SSG offered to come on his day off to observe. He was politely helpful. He gained my attention, and ultimately, we produced a verbal relationship. One in which we chatted socially and superficially. Until that one moment, where one of us crossed that line to feel out the situation. And we did. Both married, we both crossed that line.

From that moment on was a relationship of seduction and secrets. I could text SSG from an empty room in the unit, beckoning him for some private fun to which he always obliged. The privacy and intimacy of it was enthralling. Eventually, brazen, unconcerned about others seeing our glances, touching our hands as we passed in the halls, or sneaking up the stairs together. SSG held parties where drinking and sex became the basis of our relationship. But I was falling hard for SSG. I would lay in bed next to him as he ran his fingers up and down my spine as he spoke sweetly to me. And I wanted to stay safely wrapped in his arms all day.

Being no longer present, and my bipolar nonsensicalness is at the helm, the period infused with alcohol, parties, sex, and fighting remains. SSG, my opposite, feeds the urge to be something other than myself. Something so distant and obsolete I bury her, then forget her. This is always about the time where what goes up must come down. Although fleeting, my current self was alive with him. He fulfilled every manic shift. Although our relationship would last for several months beyond this point, it would never be the same.

It's true what they say. If you're considerably intoxicated and then provocatively dance with a man, you're not a victim of any lude crimes. No isn't no if you look like a hoe (maybe a new military cadence?). While attending training in Alabama, that is exactly what happened to me. Yes, I was manic. Yes, I was with a group of others and willingly entered the hotel room of my attacker. Yes, I was drunk, and yes, I danced with him provocatively. What I didn't say was, just because I danced or flirted with you means I want to fuck you.

You know, patriarchal bullshit gave him the indication it was now his right. Like the saying "I took her to dinner; now she owes me." My attacker kept me hanging in conversation, waiting for everyone else to leave. I trusted him for some reason and lacked critical decision making skill through drunkenness. When the last two women left, and the door closed behind them, he pushed me to the bed and began forcefully kissing me. He positioned himself in a way he was too heavy to move or kick. In my drunken stupor I could barely move my arms. I began trying to plead with him. "Please, I just want to go home." He remained silent as he kissed all over my neck, his hands going back and forth from my breasts to my pants, tugging at my zipper.

"Please, let me go." I reiterated those words several times before there was a knock at the door. It startled him and he jumped up. Adrenaline had me right behind him. He opened the door, and it was the two women that had left earlier. They apparently held some negative feelings and were concerned enough to return and check on me. I'm certain if they hadn't, he would have raped me. I ran out the door as quickly as I could, even leaving my cell phone behind.

The shame and guilt for putting myself in that position was immediate. The next day I went to the Sergeant First Class in charge and explained what had happened. Genuinely concerned an assault had taken place, he sent me to the MPs. After their conclusion, based solely off my actions and witness accounts, there was no wrongdoing on my perpetrator's part. He was simply taking what he deserved with all the drinking and dancing. I needed to feel safe again. I needed that emotional blanket of authority to save me. I begged SSG to personally drive to Alabama to shield me from my shame. Being the man that he was he did just that. SSG had an innately good heart.

Out of what I believe was concern, SSG simply steered me in the direction of the unseen and disregarded. In my best interest, of course. And the incident was never mentioned again by him or me. Later when I went back to retake the training course, the same Sergeant First Class in charge, very matter of fact, said, "Let's hope he [commanding officer] doesn't know you're here. He is still pissed off from the last time." And just like that, my attacker was the victim, and I was the perpetrator. Again.

I was unraveling, my mania manifesting just as I explained earlier. Fun and fearless, too full of emotion, and reckless behavior was all beginning to decline once more. I recall when it all permanently went south with SSG. I was now separated from my third husband. SSG and I intentionally attended this training together. It was past my manic months now. I was increasingly volatile, rages of anger, bouts of bulimia, extreme, debilitating depression, and paranoia fueled my mental confusion with one bad decision after another.

My children had informed me that my third husband had abandoned them at home alone, leaving my oldest son, seventeen, to run the household while I was gone. My monsters were happily toying with my sanity. I was to meet SSG's family. There were plans for us to spend time together, and it was all so good. And good can't happen. Not in my psychological condition.

I sat in my hotel room as I watched *Eat Pray Love* and pretended to not here SSG bang on my door begging me to open and speak to him. Tears streaming down my face, I was frozen. I tucked my knees up into my chest with my arms wrapped around them and buried my head. I drank in excess, called another man, and finally created circumstances in which SSG could enter my room. Coincidence, not at all. It was hard. I didn't want to be doing this, but I had no choice. Even in my drunken stupor, even with the other man on the phone, I was telling SSG, "I am sorry." That I meant. But like my first husband, SSG and I were both walking pipe bombs, both with inescapable demons. Me through my mental illness, and SSG through numerous deployments causing significant PTSD, with alcohol front and center.

In full bipolar fashion, there was a dramatic departure on my part. When I'm constantly crossing and teetering lines of permanent dissolution and heightened loss of control, nothing ends amicably when I'm despondent or manic. There is never a soft landing. Do I even care anymore? I can't remember. Facing my consequences, SSG moved on quickly, as he should've. I reconciled with my third husband for the last time, then discharged a year early from the Army, honorably.

My employment was also devastatingly affected by the sudden cyclic upshifts in my persona. Yet somehow mania was more conducive to promotion. It helps when you are charming and have an intuitive nature on reading people. This gives you a leg up on communicating effectively to those around you in a way they respond. When working for a tire company, I had a boss who was very carefree in life. Although he was structured, organized, and had excellent leadership qualities, he wanted to enjoy every moment of every second in between work. He loved the mantra "work smarter, not harder."

This I appreciated and shared. I moved up from warehouse expeditor, driving a forklift and loading trucks, to his administrative assistant after taking a long leave to work alongside SSG earlier. When I returned, this is when Bob, my boss, and me began really getting to know each other. Maybe for me, I was also attracted to his level of authority. His authority and attention in turn gave me a level of authority and respect. In addition, it gave me a level of validation in my work and as an employee. Bob took interest in teaching me as much as he could about the company we worked for; more so, his tactics as a leader.

Bob ultimately promoted me to national account manager. He trusted me to handle a myriad of tasks, more than I believed in myself. I created and implemented the first multi-state truck route for a new national account. He gave me oversight of our new drivers, and I prepared scrap-outs for customers to go over their tire failure assessments—as well as traveling regularly to make visible contact with customers and last-minute deliveries.

He became a best friend; I think because he was just as dysfunctional as I am. I won't say it was a particularly healthy relationship all the time, but he never wavered when my mental state ebbed and flowed. He was always there to open the door to his Jeep so we could hit the road and forget the rest. This allowed my shifts to go unnoticed as an employee. When I was manic, I would go all in with ideas, thoughts, and advice. When I was down, I didn't have to apologize for it; I could just sit back and let Bob take charge. We went to small bars in obscure towns off the beaten path, spent rainy days on a bar patio, held deep conversations about life while hitting the scenic byways. It was a fruitful arrangement for both of us.

This didn't bode well in future employment. The second tire company I worked for did not have a Bob. I did have a supervisor who took interest in me because his personality was that of resident cheerleader. He saw the good in everything. And wanted to see it in everyone. Always standing up for his crew. Always available for additional training and insights. However, here I was responsible to a standard at all times. Unlike with Bob, I was a hired friend with benefits, the benefit being I worked from time to time. Here, I actually had to show a visible work ethic with no disruptions.

Manic, I landed this job by making direct eye contact with confidence, thus giving them confidence in me. It was an easy sell. Unfortunately, I took this job in August, so by September I was already declining—the beginning of the darkest depression I have ever experienced. When I couldn't ride the coattails of my initial drive, I asked to be demoted to sales counter, on the guise I wanted additional training. Not quite a year later, while I was in full manic form again, an internal sales position became available.

Feeling genuinely able to do whatever I set into motion, the interview was easy. And I was once again promoted. In this role, the many faces of mania took a turn. I believe this to be a result of environmental factors as much as biological. The biological clock and mood are already there, but situations provide how it displays from one moment to another. I was past grandiose, euphoria, but stuck in hyperactive, sleep-deprived, and beginning agitation.

With this role came an office. The office was between two doorways, where people from the warehouse area could, if they needed to, walk through my office into another meeting room that led outside.

There were also two other entrances. Misophonia began to set in. This was an emotional and physical response to sounds around me, such as typing on a keyboard, yawning, and even breathing. It created a response of rage, the need to escape or do something aggressive. I could actively create visions in my mind of smashing coffee cups over someone's head, slamming their fingers in drawers, stabbing them with pencils, or tripping them as they walk by.

In particular, one warehouse employee repeatedly opened the door through my office, unnecessarily, numerous times a day. I ranted to the operations manager and demanded a sign be placed on that door. EMERGENCY EXIT ONLY. In an effort to shut me up from my tirade, he hesitantly agreed. I believe it was the second time this gentleman walked through that door despite the sign that I was in full fight or flight.

The door swung open, and I jumped up from my desk screaming, "IS THERE A FIRE??" He was clearly confused, so I clarified. "THAT IS AN EMERGENY EXIT! THERE MUST BE AN EMERGENCY! IS THERE A FIRE? SOMEONE GET THE FIRE ALARM!" All eyes were now on me. This warehouse worker caught off guard, maybe a little embarrassed, immaturely said, "I don't care what that sign says. I will do whatever I want." He then stormed away in protest.

In under fifteen minutes, the operations manager, who had just spoken to the now disgruntled warehouse worker, had an entire crew of mechanics packing up my office. He was throwing me out of the building and moving me to a sister location a few blocks away. In some cases, what I did would warrant disciplinary action. But this was a prime example of how the initial manic motivation gave me continued clout.

Even as I sat with no office, no phone, and no computer in my new building accommodations, the vice president and my direct supervisor apologized to me for the actions of the operations manager, then took me to lunch. I was given the best corner office in the building and told to keep up the good work. How, you ask? Because I was still riding the coattails of my initial impressive work ethic that allows me to slack when things got south. This has an expiration date.

Time passed on bare minimum. Before, I had to demote myself to avoid further suspicion. This time I was able to stay just under the radar until my next manic episode. And when that one hit, it was a doozy. The sun hits my skin, it seduced me into feeling unstoppable yet again. It fills my pores with intense energy, enthusiasm, and determination. Here we go. I'm feeling at the prime of my health. I look good and feel good. I owed it to the world to share this being I call me. I needed to do something, make a change, be creative!

There it was, right in front of me, an email that the marketing director out of the Omaha branch had resigned. So, what if I knew nothing about marketing. This was happening. I needed this job to prove I was intelligent, capable, articulate, and, well, amazing enough to pull this off. In my usual uninterrupted mode of manic-crazed research, I watched as many videos on digital marketing as I could. I read article after article, reviewed every website and literature from other tire and oil companies, then prepared my marketing proposal.

Within one week I submitted my resume, cover letter, and marketing proposal to the company president. Within two days he acknowledged me directly, and the following week interviewed me in person. Twenty-four hours later, I was the new marketing director. I winged it, stayed online, offered up digital marketing ideas, and created a company newsletter. In my chronic sleepless drive, I discovered overpayments in the thousands, per month, to a company managing the website. I then fired them and took over the website myself.

This position was fun; it offered an outlet to my creative side. I excelled and gained an enormous amount of knowledge in a short period of time. Then it was gone. A position like this doesn't offer a down cycle. You are either in or out. You are either performing or you're not. I had gone as far as I could go. I couldn't demote again. Paranoia set in hard and fast. I couldn't function for a day at work without hearing voices in the hall, speaking about me. I neurotically identified every facial expression and body language as an assault on my character. I did the only thing I could do. Run.

After gaining word that my bosses were on to my lack of performance lately, I quickly resigned. It is what I do best. When things get tough, go. Even in my first position, when Bob left the company and I couldn't join his new team, I left the one we worked together. This is a common theme. Not just in employment, but relationships, and more. Typically, it's the paranoia that seeps in and speaks pain into my mind. "You're worthless and stupid." "They're all onto you." "You can't measure up to anything." "Just quit; it's easier." It is in fact easier.

Some of what I tell myself is engrained through upbringing. Although I have an amazing relationship with my mother now, she used to lack the innate maternal nurturing that comes so easy for many mothers. She, like her own mother, was very critical. It was easier to know what she didn't appreciate about me than what she did. It was easier to understand what she expected of me that I failed to meet. And in no attention, she offered lack of affection and feelings of inadequacy.

What I mean by that is, we didn't speak about anything important to my future. Not college, not finances, not boys, not my period, not sex. Nothing. I had no expectation going into the world with no understanding of what was to come. I had no goals for higher learning or the future at all, for that matter. Where I ended up was simply what happened along the way of existing.

This dictated that I was a failure, constantly only capable of making mistakes. Always criticized and never validated for positives. I used to think she didn't want me to succeed because she herself felt inferior. Keeping me down meant she could always feel above me, always picking up my pieces, then holding them over me. Appearing as the savior to my children and those around me. Her words and the feelings they left me reside permanently in the voices of my monsters. Expelled through my paranoia. I know this not to be true now, but this is what my monsters showed me for years.

There are so many other consequences to mania; too many to put into one book. I want to convey that mania is not always the same. It doesn't look alike for everyone. Mania can manifest and change. What I do know is, everyone loves a manic girl…until she's not. She is an exuberant light to every party. She is the doting new lover, always ready to give of herself. She is the glance of hope to friends and family for a life less dark. She is the mother at attention always ready for fun after every shitstorm. It's all a façade. Temporary in nature. As quickly as she arrives, she departs.

Everyone loves a manic girl

Always the life of the party
Hyper-sexualized feeling naughty
This seductive confidence is only a ruse
She laughs with vigor while she holds her liquor
So that any man can unzip her jeans
An inner drive to be divine and thin
She feels free to shed her skin
With anyone who's not deserving of her within
There's no sleep while her rapid thoughts
Come to exhaust her friends and family
Money is no object especially when no one else objects
Everyone loves a manic girl
Her creativity comes with profound ease
Swimming like crashing tides colliding in her mind
The lock to her inner vault is insecure
Her mind free to take in the world
Without cognitive impairment, I can show you what I've
    really got
I'm not a stupid girl, I'm truly not
The whiplash from the crash puts me back in place
Picking up the pieces without a warm embrace
What have I done, what a disgrace
Everyone loves a manic girl
Until she's not

TWELVE

Meeting My Monster Slayer

Exactly one year to the day of my move to the country, I was unpacking once again. My now adult oldest son stayed with my third husband, while my three youngest moved with me in town. Although each fresh slate was shrouded in mania, this one was inevitable. My new place signified a clean slate. Putting things together, each in its place, with my personal touch, felt liberating and unimpeded.

Full of energy, a break was warranted. I was just a block from the bustling festivities of another July Fourth celebration. The sound of the laughter, sweet smells, and friends nearby enticed me toward the celebration. The same food trucks appeared, only this time I could smell the funnel cakes from my front door. Craft booths, rides, and more lined the streets in their annual dedication. I could hear the gleeful crowd humming in my direction. Walking in that direction felt lighter and carefree. On the surface I was utterly unburdened.

While serving in the Army, I met Kenneth, Mr. Square Jawline. A polite guy, southern drawl, and an Olympic talker. On a bus traveling for hours, he was a great seatmate to keep the ride interesting and to pass time quickly. He was a very sweet guy, very family oriented, loved his wife and children. He did appreciate the opportunity to ask a woman about topics related to marital struggles. I gladly offered my very dysfunctional advice. Over a Valentine's Day during drill, I helped him select the perfect ring for his wife at a local department store. Kenneth was the type of guy so different than me; I would have never intentionally planned to see him again.

Nevertheless, it doesn't matter how far you travel. The universe will catch up to you. The previous year, while my youngest daughter was on the Ferris wheel and my husband at my side, Mr. Square Jawline caught my eye as I heard his voice. Ironically, he was a police officer in my new small town. We acknowledged one another, made simple pleasantries, then a brief introduction to my husband and son standing nearby. I politely said something along the lines of "see you around" before walking off to take in the rest of the sites. For a year, I never saw him again.

Yet there he was, right in front of me, same day a year later, in the exact same location.

He suddenly appeared a lot more attractive than I remembered. I just left my third husband and he just separated from his wife. I offered to be an ear, a common bond to bring us together in an effort to be a shoulder for one another. He teases me to this day about my flirting tactics.

Entirely unlike my past relationships, Kenneth turns out to be forever charming, always checking on me, texting, or calling. Stopping by to bring me flowers, coffee, or love notes. Attentive and in tune with every mood. I should be envisioning dates out with my new prince charming more along the lines of dinner, picnics, movies, live bands, or strolls in quaint shopping districts while licking ice cream and romanticizing about the future.

This was not our courting period. As weeks went on and the thrill of mania left with it, my dear new boyfriend, in uniform just off a night shift, sat with me at an urgent care mental health clinic. He held my hand while I cried and bit my nails. Not to mention picking me up off the floor wrapped in my shower curtain after passing out from a new medication. He never skipped a beat, never questioned me, never wavered in his determination to date me. This I couldn't understand. Although he was literally conveying every characteristic of the affectionate lover I needed, it also proved to be too much at times.

I embarked on a yo-yo pattern, taking him all in, then pushing him away. So many critical reasons for this current behavioral instability. Still processing the loss of my previous husband. Even though I ended it, moving on from someone's long-term presence is difficult. Second, embedded learned responses from my past. The need to be cold and disconnected in an effort to protect my own ego. Third, the current declining state of my mental health. And fourth, our obvious and direct differences. From religion, to politics, upbringing, and age. Even sometimes struggling with his country-bumpkin aesthetics. I was vain.

I wasn't the only one. He too was fresh from a relationship, and although showing an enormous amount of investment in me as a future partner, had reservations. After he had been cheated on, being hurt will do that to you. Insistent was every astrological sign, universal pull, and lunar influence shouting we were meant to be together. And we knew it too. In my condition, it felt divine; it felt written in stone. I needed him. We needed each other.

I have never felt love in the way Kenneth shows it to me. I spent years of feeling incomplete, always searching for this blank space to be filled. Always seeking something or someone that would console my pain and tell me everything would be okay. Not a savior; a partner. Kenneth, my monster slayer, is the presence that I needed in order to see my way through every episode. My monsters feared his presence; they feared the strength I could gain from his support. With every embrace, kiss, I love you, and expression of encouragement.

Journal Entry
August 20, 2016

The monster in my head is punching me in the gut, it is punishing me
"Do you feel that" it rumbles
"Yes" I whisper weakly "I feel it"
It's taunting me, it wants me to lash out, be destructive and ruin another relationship. It makes me say such terrible things. Again, my conscious mind cries for me. It cries, so I cry. Every word I hear is processed in my mind as if my worst enemy is confronting me. Don't speak don't approach me. I am disoriented. The innocent faces create a disruption.

I challenge my mind long enough to push the monster back, even if only for a moment I put on my façade long enough to handle my obligations. This exhausts me. It's as if any power I have against the darkness is depleted leaving me limp and debilitated. Every ounce of energy has been spent. I sleep until the next obligation, and I will do it all over again.

My conscious mind remains persistent, "You love them, they are innocent, you have a good life, and you are happy here."

Journal Entry
August 21, 2016

    As I lay asleep utterly drained from all signs of life, the monster pummels my body in a sadistic way. It circled me like a tornado, punching me in the head neck, and shoulders. It spun around in my gut twisting into a figure-eight loop. It held its thumbs firmly into my eyes with an unrelenting pressure.

    I wake in excruciating pain. Despite that I cannot recall it, I know what it has done, as it has every dark season in the past. My muscles stiff and bruised. My stomach so agitated I will not eat. Pain radiating from the back of my neck to my temples. And my eyes sensitive to all light. Today I am no match for its reigning terror over me physically and emotionally. Today I remain weak.

Journal Entry
August 22, 2016

My monster slayer

He is a cop, it's in his blood. I hope the monster can sense his strength. Whether I wake suddenly frightened from the visions the monster flashes in my head, or I lay there battered, weak, and full of tears. My monster slayer gently approaches me, he calmly and smoothly moves the disheveled hair from my eyes and around my face. He kisses my forehead, wraps his arms tightly around me and whispers in my ear. It's as if he is speaking directly to my monsters, "My angel, have I told you today how beautiful you are?" "Have I told you how much I love and adore you?" "You are my beautiful angel."

In my mind, he tells the monsters that I am his, that I'm an angel. Not a broken and weak creature the monster wants of me. A cocktail of endorphins, dopamine, and serotonin rushes my body, drowning the monsters temporarily, feeling an overwhelming sense of security and and peace. It quiets my mind, and I wish to wear him like a suit of armor each day.

Journal Entry
August 24, 2016

    The monster has distorted my vision with his continual nightly attacks. My eyes so battered by my darkness I am unable to see clearly or sharply. Each line of every image slightly frayed. I blink and wince praying each time I reopen it will be restored. Upon looking into the mirror at myself, my eyelashes now a solid line, the curves to my nostrils indistinct. I am unable to make out the individual hairs from my eyebrows that usually dance in fullness from my brow bone. Chaos already marked me deep within the posterior capsule of my right eye in the womb. A circular cataract is too intricate in its placement to remove and now my brain is unable to work in partnership with my eyes' ability to make any natural corrections over time. Any new disturbances are significant given my already limited visibility, particularly now present in my primarily healthy left eye.

THIRTEEN

What Would My Letter Say?

Now in my forties, my monsters were significantly bound to tearing me apart from the inside out. Corrupting my mind first, then watching my shell deteriorate in a snowball effect I had never experienced before. No divorce, no stint in a drunk tank, no other road of upheaval to date prepared me for bipolar and aging. A swell of sadness consumed my being.

After months of skimming by on looks and lies at work, I was unable to leave my bed let alone get in my GPS-tracked vehicle to show some work initiative. Not at first. I determined just how much and how far I needed to travel to keep suspicions at bay. The melancholy was so deep that in my travels I parked near bodies of water, contemplating a plunge. How fast would I have to be in order to get a distance far enough that the water would flood over my head?

I never wondered about the pain of taking in the water. The image was always peaceful and without suffering. When I envisioned the scene, it was of soft polite waters filling up around my body, each inch removing a little more suffering. Even as it engulfed my shoulders, then my face, and over my head, there was no fear. Only an absence of pain. There were some thoughts of the end, less consolatory. Driving under bridges stirred appearances of my body frightfully falling from the ledge, either directly into the fire of traffic or from a noose where my body would bounce against the rope when it met its length.

As time moves, Christmas comes and goes. New Year's proves to be the gateway to another twelve-month session of sinister context. Spring upon me, and I await with anticipation, mania. It never comes. Never rising for its obligatory presence. Delighting my monsters, darkness remains to my discomposure. How much of me must they consume before there's nothing left? Do they want me dead? There's an inappreciable sense of liberation toward my demise slithering into my consciousness.

Summer offers no solace either as the contemplation of my liberation becomes easier to envision. Not only easier but gratifying. I rationalize my departure, convincing myself that each person in my life is at a stage in which the impact of a loss would be less grievous. New torments present. Waking from full rem sleep fixed upright, panicked, hysterical, and sobbing, with no memory of the horror that tormented me. Comforted by the arms of my boyfriend, my monster slayer.

How will I do it? The most important question when idealizing suicide. More so than when or where. When my boyfriend and I moved in together, so did his gracious array of police gear, including several firearms. One in particular, always kept tucked under his side of the mattress, a black Glock 17, 9mm. Fitting pleasantly in my petite hands. Coaxed by my monsters, compelled to feel the pressure of the cool barrel on my warm temple. I feel the weight of the gun in my hands, my finger on the smooth curve of the trigger. I put the gun to my head, I take a deep breath in, then exhale. I am not afraid.

There is a deep disconnect for people who experience suicide in some six degrees of separation. It presents the common feeling of being unable to comprehend the state of mind of the person who took their own life. I hope through my experience you can at least understand one perspective. The demons make death feel peaceful and yes, even liberating. After this very conversation with my boyfriend, I decided to write what my suicide letter would have said, graduating to a more poetic version.

RIVKA M. STIEH

What Would My Letter Say?

Imprisoned by false pain, feeling absolutely insane
The monsters in my brain manipulated my perception
And for that, I always caused so much negative projection
I don't deserve forgiveness just because of my sickness
It doesn't matter anyway
The incessant chatter in my mind, in many ways, is a cold
    dark bind
It never ceases to exist, my conscious soul always dismissed
Paranoia, guilt, shame, sadness, and overall madness is all
    I feel
I know now I may never heal
I beg for freedom from the insanity
It overshadows all the love and humanity
I love you all with every ounce of me
But it isn't enough to quiet my reality
Please forgive me for my fall
I know not how to uninstall
The constant voices in my head
Always filling me with dread
I'm at peace now, knowing I'll be free
And now you no longer have to worry about me

FOURTEEN

Turn of Events

My father died. The death of a loved one will certainly impose questioning your mortality. Everything seems different, like new rose-colored lens filters. The idea of legacy, what you leave your family with to talk about at holiday dinners, family reunions, and birthdays, becomes relevant. My stepfather had the kind of legacy people will admire for the ages. He lived out of cars and tents as a child, joined the circus as a pre-teen. His stories were grand. They were emotional and something straight out of a Rick Bragg novel. Yet he rose to the top with nothing more than an eighth-grade education through pure will and determination. Talk about overcoming your odds.

I stand in front of the podium exhausted and torn apart as I deliver my father's eulogy before four hundred people who have all come to know and adore him. They respected him as a selfless fireman, a headstrong politician, and a man revered for all his works as a public servant. Having written his eulogy in under forty-eight hours, I am surprised by the raw emotion I invested in it. It was not a contrived mechanical purging of his life. Rather an emotional ride into his legacy as someone who had risen from the dirt during the Great Depression, to president pro-tem of a state senate.

I drew them in and gave them a glimpse of how hard he worked to arrive at such stature and boasted of his successful life. I wrapped it up with statements regarding my ability to test his patience as the brooding teenager and more recently an unkempt adult. After all, I was the child that emotionally spewed my lies as he lay unconscious on his deathbed. "Dad, I'm so sorry, I spent all the bankruptcy money you gave me!" And in front of this audience, through sobs as I looked up into the church ceiling, to thank my deceased father. "Thank you, Dad, for loving me even when I was unlovable."

After everyone departed the church, we retreated to my parents' home for an intimate reception with close family and friends. I stood in the corner of the living room slightly into the hallway just out of sight, observing my mother and children. Is this the scene I want for them to experience all over again? Seems my liberation is now tied to further victimization. The motive now, immaterial. They would only attempt to forget how I left them, by remaining steadfast in their silence, oppressing their grief. I don't want this.

Journal Entry
August 27, 2016

My father died this morning. I woke suddenly in bed around 4 am. Within minutes my mother calls me, then tells me calmly he passed sometime between 3-4 am. Maybe he was notifying me subtly through the universe.

Of course, I go to her. I find my darkness gives me some solitude. I am able to express emotions, provide some support, and kick into full gear to do whatever my mother needs of me today.

Journal Entry
August 29, 2016

Today I was diagnosed with Central Serous Retinopathy in my good left eye. With the trauma induced cataract behind my right eye, this makes my current vision very diminished. My physician says my right eye has no options, even surgery won't guarantee any success. Then he tells me amblyopia prevented it from trying to correct itself over the years. A brain disconnect of some sort.

He goes on to tell me the causes of CSR are a bit of a mystery. I envision my monsters pressing into my eyes. He also tells me that they know stress is a contributing factor. Thinking of my darkness, my father's death, and my recent desire to die, I resign myself to life of poor vision.

Journal Entry
August 30, 2016

My aggressive side of mania begins to hit in full swing today over the fit and feel of a new bra. I began an extreme panic of feeling constricted, the monsters whisper in my ear, "you are a fat disgusting slob, you'll always be disgusting." I repeat it out loud as I stormed around looking for one of my only comfortable broken in bras. I paced, stormed, slammed doors, spoke to myself in a hostile and derogatory way.

I wanted so badly to break things, hit something, especially myself. I wanted to feel the pain I deserve for being so disgusting. Pacing with shallow breaths, I beg it to stop. I mutter to myself, "Not now, I can't do this now."

I didn't want my boyfriend to see me like this. He has seen my sadness, but never the anger or my delusional thoughts and perceptions.

Moments like these, deep with disgust, anger, and the desire to hurt myself, being something, I hate, one more trigger could open death's door. I mentally shoot myself on repeat. I just want it to end. I am so tired of the struggles. My darkness is exacerbated, relentless, a river of drama that all leads back to me. I don't do enough, save enough, spend too much, don't make enough, my dad died, my car is in the shop, my son's car needs repairs, the kids need lunch money, I missed their school pictures, bounced a check, and have no food. That is just this week.

I just want to pull the trigger, then I would be free of the constant reminders of where I fail and disappoint all my life.

Journal Entry
September 1, 2016

Don't fucking touch me.

The flip switched during dinner. I was able to stave it off long enough to get out the door. I didn't want my family to recognize the change in my demeanor. I was quick, I went from feeling solemn, yet social, to cold and angry with intense pressure in my chest. The longer I held the rage in the more intense it felt. It radiated from my stomach with instant nausea. I wanted to leave immediately.

I entered the car with my dear boyfriend. I was so on edge. Every noise or touch, signing to the radio, nail biting, his hand on my knee has me violently mentally slamming my face on the dashboard over and over again. I could only make the drive by taking deep breaths, keeping my eyes closed, and mentally willing away the darkness. I wouldn't let my monsters make me act out this way. I wanted so badly to scream, hit something, smash something, anything to release the violence.

Home, two Ativan later, my mind is quiet, and so am I.

Journal Entry
September 6, 2016

Welcome Paranoia.

This is the side of the dark season I almost dread more than anger or sadness. Paranoia will literally make you feel crazy. My mind is attempting to interpret everything as suspicious. Everyone's actions from facial expressions to body language are perceived as negative and my instinct is to prepare for fight or flight. This is the phase throughout history I have historically quit jobs because I am convinced, they will fire me anyway. Or exit a relationship because, well, why not. They do not love me anyway. As if they are twins, paranoia always comes with self-loathing. I am literally disgusted at the mere thought of my physical self. And with that comes rejection of love. Dear boyfriend senses my hesitations and instinctively attempts to draw me in closer. I become so uncomfortable with every look, comment of adoration, and touch. I physically withdrawal and shutter inside. I whisper to myself as if it is a new mantra, please do not touch me, please do not touch me, please do not touch me. I fear if he glances at me, he will notice some hideous flaw and react. The monster within me is laughing. It is telling me how everyone finds me repulsive, that I should be repulsed, that no one loves me, and I am not worthy of love. That everyone is judging me.

I retreat into the darkness...shaming myself, protecting myself from everyone and from anyone seeing me. The monster is winning today, but I am conscious enough to understand despite how I feel, this is not rational. It may win today, but I will win this war.

Journal Entry
September 7, 2016

I'll take your paranoia and self-loathing and add anger, hostility, and resentment.

My skewed perception is getting the better of me. I am somehow stuck in fight or flight. Well, primarily fight. Everyone and everything are causing me to act aggressively. My poor dear children can do nothing right, and I chastise them relentlessly. My dear boyfriend is probably doing something wrong, so I react in a very methodical passive-aggressive manner. Some of my coworkers are lazy, lack structure, and require discipline so I respond with pure agitation. There is a knot of pure hate deep within my chest. It's as if the monster has grabbed my heart with its cold dead hand and stopped it from beating. Another day lost to the darkness. Please, God, put your warmth and loving kindness in my heart today. Bring it back to life with calming peace.

Journal Entry
September 13, 2016

Death is at the forefront of my mind as I face yet another goodbye today.

My dear boyfriend's mother passed away at 1:55 am. The most difficult part of all of this is my father's death is still fresh and it continues to drudge up all the sadness and grief.

As I sit here feeling completely disconnected, I fear I will not be the support system my dear boyfriend needs and deserves. I cannot muster up emotion and the more he talks about his the more uncomfortable I remain.

Since the monster has stripped me of all feelings, I am helpless. I know how I should feel, how I should react, but...nothing. Maybe it is safer this way. I will continue to profess my love and remain a diligent listener.

Journal Entry
September 16, 2016

I am feeling so anxious, uptight, sick to my stomach, jealous, nervous and paranoid. It seems from nowhere, but my intuitive nature is keen. I feel my dear boyfriend is pulling away from me.

FIFTEEN

Frenzied Spiritual Fascination

My monsters are incessant. Always reminding me of my imperfections. To date, I managed to stave off following through with suicide. How does someone like me, someone often in a condition of self-destruction, teetering death, facing so much wickedness still find an inkling of hope? Is it sudden divine intervention? Or my resolute need to seek spiritual repentance?

In a tornado of moods, in rapid succession, both gravely melancholic and insidiously manic. I have been known to chase down every obsessive narrative leading to a higher power. Every dot connects in synchronicity. Every move appears to be not of chance, bringing me to something bigger than myself. I chase it like a vein chasing metal, pushing that fire-and-ice, chemically induced euphoria. Like Mel Gibson chasing conspiracies. Like a mad scientist pushed to the extreme.

Mania isn't just about careless spending, heightened sex impulses, excessive drinking, obsessive dieting, and impulsive life choices.

Chasing every whim with the tenacity of a crack addict. It's also defined by the part of me desperately seeking solace, a cure for the wickedness manning my brain. Like the addict, I'm all in. A temporary driving force to my existence. Repeatedly throwing myself into religion. The mysticism of some power so great it creates miracles. So powerful the majority of the world follows blindly. More importantly, it is forgiving. It is the redemption and enlightenment I seek.

Jew"ish"ness

Bouts of desire for Temple and a renewed faith in Judaism. Contemplating head coverings to prove I can be modest, not a whore. As a child, I attended a large synagogue with a multitude of classrooms and a sizable temple for service. I especially recall the music room because it was bright and inviting with beautiful stained-glass windows. Its light wooden pews amid the center of the synagogue near an atrium that was angelic with natural light. And although it was not the quiet of the woods that I had begun to feel drawn to, it offered music, and to me, this was the best part of Sunday school. The songs were upbeat and cheery, everyone always smiling and happily swaying to the beat of the acoustic guitar notes. One way to leave a small trinket of positive remembrance associated with Temple.

As a family dedicated to the yearly rituals of Passover and Hanukkah, we dabbled in the high holy days of Rosh Hashanah and Yom Kippur, the day of atonement. We did things like building the Sukkot with classmates in autumn to commemorate the sheltering of the Israelites in the wilderness. We ate apples with honey on Rosh Hashanah, the Jewish New Year. Outside of Temple, we rarely participated in anything particularly Jewish. We didn't adhere to the laws of Shabbat or keep kosher. We didn't read from the Tanakh, nor did we discuss scriptures or bible stories as a family. We identified as Reform Jews. I call us Jew"ish."

When I was married to my third husband, often manically prompted by some source of motivation, I began to spend many days, weeks, and months in spiritual self-reflection. While in basic training I committed myself every Sunday to taking a bus on post to a Jewish synagogue for prayers of self-condemnation and guilt. Once home, I picked up more books on Judaism to hone in on things I could do to bring myself closer to Him.

I needed rituals that would help me with moral strength. I clung to a Jewish prayer book I had received from an Army chaplain who was drawn to me during a weekend weapons qualification. He was curious about my upbringing in Judaism, and I indulged his conversation. In turn he graciously mailed me two Jewish bibles and the prayer book I now always carry. One page creased, folded at the tip, and the spine already broken down to the exact spot of that page, the prayer for moral strength.

There were times when I began inconsistent periods of honoring the Sabbath with candles and prayer. I started reading the Jewish prayers to myself and my children before bed and meals. I thought at the time this would make me more pleasing to God, allowing me to feel more comfortable in my own skin. I researched Jewish women and how to reflect modesty. I delved into learning more in depth about the rituals of Yom Kippur. I felt confident this would be the way to my redemption.

After I had left my third husband for the last time, in my usual methodology, I dove right into repentance, blanketing my guilt with a temporary religious expression to God. Yom Kippur waits for me every September, knowing I will require forgiveness after the dust of the previous spring and summer mania settles. Focused on the formalities and rigidity of the rules to ensure better success that God will open His book and put my name inside, I work on my apologies. This time, with a more sincere and dire need. I construct one letter, each suited for those deserving.

There's no such thing as collateral damage when it comes to your children. They weren't in the wrong place at the wrong time. Whether conscious or unconscious elements, it's a decision to engage in factors that will affect their lives forever. Nothing you do can undo what was done. But I try anyway. With all the love in my being, I won't ever stop trying. Young children will remain steadfast in their love for you, but a time will come in their early adult lives when they realize things weren't quite normal, and their distance will break your heart.

I began my amends to each of my children individually. I calculated how each one in their unique personality would better accept such a conversation. I chose to begin in chronological order and reached out to my oldest son. He was twenty-one and hands down the most financially responsible, definitely a natural worrier, and undoubtedly an introvert. He inevitably clinged to money since I took a more fly-by-the-seat-of-my-pants approach to finances. He works in an isolated job, restores Fox Body Mustangs as an enthusiast, does stock trading over the internet, has vowed to more than likely never marry—and most certainly never have children.

He only occasionally leaves the confines of his own bedroom and computer chair to socialize with longtime childhood friends. The friends who are entirely accustomed to his lack of filter or inability to mince words. He is most certainly a straight shooter. Just ask my good friend Nicole, who ran into him while shopping at the local Dollar General.

Nicole saw him in an aisle and happily looked to him with a "Hey, how are you, Nathan?" To which my son responded quietly, "I literally don't know who you are." Flabbergasted by his brutal honesty and lacking some tact, Nicole immediately chose to do an about-face, avoiding any more awkwardness. My son later told me as she turned away, he tried to redeem the situation, but it was too late. At least he recognized the non-verbal facial clue she had so evidently displayed in response.

My son partially gets the solitude from his father, but it is my guilt that convinces me it is a deep-seated insecurity in which I created as a result of his unpredictable upbringing. I figure he must consciously or subconsciously feel it is best to remain isolated than put himself out there for people who could possibly let him down. Or even worse, reject him as he felt so rejected as a child, crying to me in the car about the repeated absence of a father. Although my son and his father now have a relationship, it has been one of little emotional acknowledgment or connection. They are two peas in a pod in this regard. It's not the kind of relationship that could unwind all that had already been done over the twenty-plus years.

With my oldest son I chose to text. I know this may seem incredibly impersonal to an outsider, but knowing him, this was the easiest way to obtain a real emotional response from the guy who typically says so little. Unless you're talking about fast cars and money. I sent him the apology in great detail about how I feel that my repeated failed marriages did not provide a suitable model of what to expect in a marriage or other potential relationships.

I expressed how saddened I was that he didn't have a loving, nurturing father figure in his life. That I couldn't imagine how that must make him feel. I let him know how I hoped he could see that in spite of the past, there is so much to look forward to in relationships with people and putting yourself out there. I told him how much I love him and admire his hard work to be a successful and financially secure adult. After I timidly hit send, I waited patiently for his response. I could not have asked for a more perfect and to-the-point reply. "I LOVE YOU" is all it said. "I love you" was all I needed from me to the point straight shooter son who still in a way wants to take care of me.

Working my way down the line, I worked up the nerve to approach my oldest daughter. My oldest daughter was always the "responsible one," a burdensome title I placed on her. A title that came with pressure and expectations. She was the dutiful daughter who didn't want to let her dysfunctional mother down. There was no room for her to stand out aside her brothers with the attention they demanded She found her voice through music and art, outlets for her secret language, expressing those suppressed emotions. She grew with a tough exterior, with little patience for drama in friendships. Too much of that at home. Always carried a disposition of anger and depression hidden behind real authentic beauty. I don't think she knows just how beautiful she is.

With my daughter away in college, I convinced myself I didn't want to impede on her newfound college life. She had only been in college a few weeks now. So, I send her my apology through Facebook messenger. With her, I was a coward. I gave her a very similar apology to my sons, adding in the need to let go of anger and allow herself to be free and enjoy life to its fullest. I read it back to myself and reread again before hitting send.

She responded first by telling me that I shouldn't apologize because she attributes all her passionate qualities to me. Can you imagine that? She so graciously told me I was the reason she was the independent, successful, and passionate woman she is today. That my toughness got her through our circumstances, not exacerbated them.

My oldest daughter is now married. She has a new life, is focused on a new career track. History has struck her more deeply. It is not uncommon for young adults facing their own life as a separate family to reflect, unwrap, and process their upbringing. I know I did. It's a difficult period shrouded in a lot of whys. My daughter carries an underlying concern for being a successful wife and future parent herself, given the toxicity of the one who raised her. What I know is that, without a doubt, she will not only be successful as a teacher, wife, and mother but dissect and separate the negative environmental ties commonly passed down in generations. Stopping them with me.

I chose to tackle my youngest son and daughter simultaneously at our tiny bistro kitchen table, a more nonchalant approach as to not stir up too much emotion in one setting. My son stood as my youngest daughter sat. I explained my reason for the conversation. That I was holding myself to Yom Kippur so that I might be forgiven for my sins and not only by God but by anyone whom I have wronged.

My youngest son is unique. He was a handful in that I reached a point in his upbringing that it was imperative I do the best I could with where I was mentally in order to create some success for him. My youngest son was hypersensitive to sounds and materials. Overstimulated to extreme highs. Clearly some miscommunication caused havoc in his frontal lobe, a shared genetic fault handed down by both biological parents. There were bouts of raging anger, from what a doctor once explained, being in fight or flight mode all the time.

When he wasn't angry, or overstimulated and hyperactive, he was completely disconnected with a deadpan face. As someone innately in tune to body language and facial expressions, I could never read him in those moments. He had been asked to leave three preschools, choked a kid out on a bus, been in numerous fights, and desperately needed an outlet. A stint in military school as well as football and rugby, two aggressive outlets, became his saviors.

Today, my youngest son is in his third year of college. He is an excellent student and still plays rugby. He is a planner, a thinker, structured, and more laid back than he used to be. We talk about the risks for alcoholism, bipolar disorder, and autism spectrum disorder in the event he may need to seek psychiatric help. I encourage him to remain in tune with his feelings and behavior. I thank God and the universe every day for where he is today.

With my youngest son, I apologize for my unpredictability. For his father not being present. I apologize for putting him through my second husband, then my third. I apologize for not protecting him from all the chaos emotionally. Positive and upbeat, he says, "Are you kidding me? I feel so spoiled." I tried so hard with him, and in turn put in a little extra too. His response was clearly from the egregious amount of time I spent hauling him to every sport and private lesson I could, giving him a place to put that anger.

Reeling from the unwarranted responses received from the oldest three, I looked to my youngest daughter, who sat for the most part silent, taking it all in. Her response seemed more in line with what I felt I not only deserved but expected. Her expressions seemed to say she really had not been able to articulate her life to date and here I was summing it up for her. It may have even been a tad of not realizing the extent of how dysfunctional our lives had been to this point. But she was certainly struggling to be a through-and-through mama's girl yet angry for all of the constant adjustments.

In her short nine years she was trying to make sense of having a father who has since created a new family, with a new wife and children, whom she visited very infrequently. She was trying to comprehend the loss of my third husband. She had endured my constant moves from home to home, landing her in five different schools and amid hundreds of new faces and friendships. I had to promise her that when we moved this last time, she would never have to go to another school district again. Despite my changing views, I will hold true to my promise.

Having taken in all I said quietly, she offered no words of encouragement or even acceptance of my apology. Instead, she looked at me with a saddened face and provides a simple "Okay." I told her I loved her and gave her a big hug, and she reciprocates with "I love you too." So, it became a mission to remove my beautiful young flower from the wall front and center. To ensure she would not be afraid of life, was involved in activities that brought her joy, and felt secure in knowing we would remain here in this town with no chance of geographical upheaval.

My youngest, now a teenager, was in every way imaginable me. With an initial debilitating sadness for her life sentence to my disease, I overcame that quickly to ensure her the opportunities that knowledge would aid her. Everything I didn't have. Her start shadowed a bit like mine. Struggles in school, considerable social anxiety, heightened emotional responses to common situations, fear with some hints of paranoia, and mood swings of depression and mild mania. Rapid speech and exacerbated energy defined her ups. Consuming sadness, fatigue, and isolation, with significant emotional sensitivity, defined her downs. Together with spirituality and my candid truth, she would conquer this disease. With considerable honesty I was forthcoming about the history of my illness. This book is more relevant now than ever.

I'M NOT AFRAID OF THE MONSTERS

Mom

Whiplash moods
Stop talking I need quiet
Screaming, raging, everything must be in its place
Too many things in this space, it must go, it all must go
High energy, impulsive short trips, shopping excursions
Laughter for days, so many smiles and memories made
Until it rains
Days in Bed agonizing over all the things said, I'm a
　　terrible mother
When will there be warmer weather
Why can't I quiet the voices in my head
Hello are you present; I don't know if I am alive or dead
My children are growing and so is the harm
Dear little ones, mine the gold memory bank when the ages
　　remind you of the coal.

It was evident I already had forgiveness from my children at that time. I needed to convey my sorrows while ensuring I wouldn't hurt them in any way again. My second need was to forgive myself and feel forgiven by God. In the end I felt neither. I tried to convince myself for days after Yom Kippur that I had done the right thing. That I was a newly forgiven soul. I even had the words "I am forgiven" tattooed in Hebrew on my forearm in celebratory fashion. But what I had really done was made a statement, a reminder, a false proclamation. This wasn't a red string I could tie on my finger as a reminder: "Hey, Rivka, you are forgiven. Remember, your arm says so." What I unknowingly and very ironically had done was this: אני סולחת לי and what this really reads is "I FORGIVE ME."

Judaism, for me now, is a cultural identity. When it is untied to my mania, it is a part of me I admire as a place in my heritage—Ashkenazi Jews who trekked here from Germany and Romania to escape persecution and certain death. That genetic psychology lays some groundwork to being a humanitarian now. For being called to speak on behalf of those oppressed, victimized, or misunderstood. Judaism is something I will always implement in areas of life. I will talk about it, continue to learn it, and pass it to my children and their children.

The Christ High

I love fall! I find the colors magnificent—the burnt oranges, deep mauves, dark greens, and hues of gold and brown. The fresh, cool air hits my face, and I breathe the crispness of it deep into my lungs, bringing me to attention. I look forward to the gleeful cheer of everyone preparing their costumes for Halloween. Followed by celebrations of thankfulness as I romanticize joyful family gatherings for Hannukah and Christmas dinner. Dining room tables adorned with festive bling, baby Jesus in a manger, a Menorah lit and glowing, Frosty the Snowman on porches, and robotic reindeer twinkling in yards. How can you not get caught up in that poetic imagery?

It was fall 2016. Feeling festive, I watched all the best of the Hallmark channel movies while caressing a forever loyal cat or two. Snuggled up in hoodie and sweatpants, tightly wrapped in a fleece blanket. Alone this evening, I was secluded not only in physical presence, but to the confines of the emotional wall I'd constructed for myself. In a tug of emptiness, I scrolled social media to feel engaged with the world.

I was half into the visual display of romantic comedies and half into the perceived representations of all my online acquaintances. Family fall photos on the backdrop of buffalo plaids, pumpkins, piles of leaves, or poinsettias. Followed by various expressions of gratitude with blessings of faith. Haphazardly liking posts of friends and family to keep myself relevant. Including shared events.

Upon liking one event, a dear friend promptly sent me a private message. She wanted to attend an event together that we had mutually submitted a liking to. Although I agreed, I felt obligated to research its speaker, whom I knew nothing about. I found that our speaker, Mrs. Zobrist, was a faith-based motivational speaker who traveled to churches speaking to other women, giving encouragement and a desire for God. I was not clear on her message, and even though my first inclination was to cancel, I didn't. This would prove to be step one in a spiritual journey, one that would begin to come to me with clarity and ease.

November 11, 2016, and in tow with two of my friends and with a slight sense of uncertainty, I was surprisingly enthusiastic to hear the speaker's message. Mrs. Zobrist was full of charisma. She was funny, relaxed, and adorable and appealed to every woman in that room. As she bounced around the stage with confidence in her message, she began laying down her spiritual information. I lacked the understanding of the biblical aspect, and the passages. I merely became enthralled in her enthusiasm for God, for life, and especially for her fellow sisters in faith.

With sweet and calming inflection in her voice, she delved into explaining that no one other than God holds authority over us, that He has already given us what we need to be Godly. That He does not guilt or manipulate. She was firm in her word to us that we have to know God, know His love, study Him, and allow Him to be our authority, trusting His word so we can be secure women.

Her words became increasingly relevant to me as I listened carefully to her insistence on understanding that with God and Christ, we have permission to stop pretending we do not have any problems. That God offers us security and permission for us to feel we are not seamless. We need to be honest with ourselves, know who we are, and what we can be capable of in pursuit of Him. We can rest in faith, be exposed, and yet still feel secure in God.

She leaned in toward the end of the stage, and with the deepest of sincerity said, "When we come to this, we can be bold and brave." She asked us to think for a moment as she now stood tall and proud with her words reflecting courage, "What passion has been laid upon your chest? What do you want to be known as?... "Your acceptance will not be found in what anyone else has to say!" She went on. "Every girl needs another girl who has her back. We need to be supporting women, not in competition. You are all one in Jesus. And it is not defined by social status, ethnicity, or gender!" Amen, sister. Amen! The words repeated in my mind like an incantation. We can REST in faith. Feel SECURE in God. Be bold and BRAVE. And I no longer have to pretend to be okay. I am not seamless. I can pursue God and find all of that. Sign me up. When do I start? How do I begin?

I had an opportunity to speak with Mrs. Zobrist after the show, and in those few moments I explained my Jew"ish"ness and how in my forty-plus years I had never felt so encouraged, so motivated. Never had I had such a desire to seek more of an understanding of Jesus. And in that moment, she grabbed me in her arms, hugged me in sheer, honest delight, and said to me, "Jesus loves you." I had heard those words before, but back then it had seemed like an auto-response that evangelical Christians overused. A slogan for a small red button. I cringed at my lack of understanding.

While growing up Jew"ish," even the mere mention of Jesus incited a visceral response of indignation. My resentment was geared more from the responses of peers, their parents, and even strangers from a highly evangelical faith-based community in which I was raised. I was commonly informed I would without uncertainty go to Hell in various lengths of description. As a young mother, many other parents continually pursued taking my children to church and groups like

Awanis. They requested it as if they were taking the poor Jewish kids to experience Christianity, saving their souls from bad parenting.

In my current intoxicated positive state, I was curious. Jesus seemed magical, the keeper of all peace, the man who created miracles. A link to freedom from everything. Financial instability, marriage strife, health ailments, grief, depression, and more. Addicts look to faith in twelve-step meetings. Prisoners find faith and baptism for forgiveness. A one-stop shop for all your woes. Is Jesus a match for my formidable monsters? The prison I was bound in was deeply woven into my entire being. I needed to know more.

Given my critically bleak year, death knocking so close to my door created an unrelenting pull to seek the wisdom of a powerful master. A force so powerful the monsters on my back faced annihilation. My soul would be saved. I sought out a pastor whose word was praised by those disenchanted by churches in the past, previously didn't believe in God, or somehow was otherwise disgruntled or uninterested.

His approach, historical insight. In his words, evidence. Pastor Ralph preached in jeans, plaid button-up shirts, and cowboy boots. From a modest church representative of a small-town farmhouse feel. White exterior, red door, black awning. Brought to life by contemporary music and Pastor Ralph's no-nonsense approach.

Fanatically, I consumed every word. Sure, he was the bringer of God. When I met him in person, he appealed to my limited understanding of the Old Testament. "I'd like to show you where in the Old Testament it talks of Jesus." He wasn't pushy, didn't criticize me into being saved so I don't go to Hell. I was already living there, nothing to lose in contemplating Christianity now. I still needed more. In my determination, I wanted this surreal, gentle seer of hope, love, perseverance, this giver of freedom to rescue me *from* me. I needed it to be true. When the pastor invited me over for a more in-depth discussion, I had to go. A culmination of impulsive drive and sheer panic for my current state of mind.

I arrived on December 15, 2016, in a bit of mixed mania. I barraged the pastor with a repetition of whys and hows. I struggled to comprehend that all of the shame, guilt, and negative mantras I'd been submerged in for so long could just be released and forgiven. In a bit of manic psychosis, I was suddenly overcome with voices, and snip-it visions of my past. "You're a deadbeat mother," my second husband said.

The monsters were taunting me; they became loud and relentless. Even in my host's calming demeanor, the darkness seeped through my mind trying to disorient me as I tried to comprehend what the pastor was saying. Maybe it was God and the evil that had taken up residence in my mind engaged in a crucial match of tug-of-war for my sanity. The voice of my father's fear: "I used to think at least you were a good mother. Now I don't even believe that…. You don't understand; she fails at everything she does."

I saw my gray lifeless infant between my shivering legs. I heard my oldest son's tears: "If this is what it's like to have a dad, I don't ever want one." Their faces, the emotions, I was right there. I saw each of my children's faces in the most vivid imagery at their most vulnerable, because of my actions. The face on my daughter Marley as she played on her floor when I interrupted to tell her I was leaving my third husband, the first time. I saw every man who victimized me and took advantage of me. I saw the look on my third husband's face when he realized I had an affair, so hurt and angry. Then saw him tear up after a weekend alone when we agreed to make it work. And again, when I disappointed him and broke my promise.

My mind was racing over the pastor's voice. Honest, he told me of his past as a rebellious youth, that we could probably go toe to toe in a list of our pitfalls and sins. That mine was no different in the eyes of God. My darkness didn't seem to weaken the pastor's unrelenting resolve to help me. I was trying to remain in disbelief, while questioning when I would know I was ready to accept Christ, for the umpteenth time. Pastor Ralph, with a sincere and earnest voice, unequivocally genuine, said, "I think you already know."

My mind suddenly quieted, and a single memory came forward. A moment when my mind was just as dissociated as it is right now. Desperate to silence the madness. I stoically submerged myself in bathwater, sinking bareback into the cold, porcelain tub, letting the water rush over my face. I heard nothing but the echoing of my deep inhales and exhales. The voices of my monsters were muffled as my breaths soothed me into deep relaxation. For that moment I felt safe. All of my sensitivities dissipated. The water was my force field from everything disturbing my mind. I didn't feel the darkness and its weight, nor its chaos. In its place was an overwhelming sense of peace and weightlessness.

This was how I felt as I looked at the pastor in that moment. My shoulders were relieved from their usual burdens. Entranced in this sudden awareness, free from the voices and memories. It must be real. On January 8, 2017, I did the only thing I knew would seal the deal. I was baptized before the church. Another all-in, following all the rules, studying, and praying frantically. All the monsters seemed absent while I rode all my manic fate on one God, one Christ, to cure me. So, what was I doing wrong?

Just under two years into our relationship my boyfriend and I married in a church. I was convinced it was what we needed in order to appease God, so I wouldn't suffer. My four children and mother, his three children, and our closest friends stood up on our behalf. Nicole and Kyle witnessed our matrimony and served as a reminder to our initial love and commitment.

Pastor Ralph began by reciting Ephesians 5:21-33 followed by an opening prayer: "Supreme Authority, preceding all other social impacts, authorized and guarded in by Civil and Divine Law, marriage cannot undergo changes from its original purpose or pass away but must remain the same and unalterable to the end of time."

To the end of time. This finally meant something to me, and I was proud and unshakable in my determination to marry this man. In my previous marriages, I never paid attention to the vows; I didn't even listen to them. But I hung on those of the pastor like I clung to everything else he had previously spoken of. I was intently focused on every single word and every syllable that came from his lips.

After reciting our vows, the pastor began his grand finale. "Then in consideration of your part of the obligations of marriage, and of your deliberate and decided choice of each other as partners in its duties and fellowship for life." I looked Kenneth in the face while consuming the pastor's words: "of your deliberate and decided choice." I could not help but relish in the word *deliberate* as this was entirely a conscious choice in clear mind, absent of any darkness.

While standing ready to accept our rings we were reminded that these bands were a representative of eternity and showed how lasting and imperishable the faith that we were pledging was. "These circles have no beginning or end. So is your love and shall continue through eternity…. It's the duty and privilege of you both, to work together, to play together, to share all things together, and to remember that in reputation as well as in affection, that in all things, you are to be undivided."

I would remember that word, *undivided*, every time Kenneth and I would ridiculously quarrel about inconsequential differences. "You are to preserve an inviolable fidelity and to see to it that what God has joined together, no one ever separates." I have never been so overcome with joy and peacefulness before a man than in that moment. I could look my monster slayer in the face and know that my new husband, a soldier of his God, would physically and emotionally protect me through darkness, love me unconditionally, and walk with me hand in hand in faith through every season in this world of this burdened body. But would it be enough?

Christ High

Searching once again for repentance on demand
So desperate for a cure so open to His word
Please let it be so
That Christ and God will let it go
I'll do anything without reason
Please exercise this melancholic demon
I caught the Christ high
Why not, I'll give it a try
They say Baptism is the medication
An organic prescription proclamation
Water, prayer, and obedience to a deity
Will my life take on a new reality?
Or will my demon seek retribution?
For yet another failed intrusion

Journal Entry
January 23, 2017

    Pray for:
    Anxiety
    Job Change
    Writing
    People to pray for:
    My children
    Kenneth
    Dear Lord in heaven,

    I pray today for comfort over anxiety, guidance for resolving anxious feelings. Lord, I ask that you show me organization, motivation, and confidence in my new position at work.

    Lord, show my children kindness and love in their hearts. Lord, I pray my mother's heart opens to your love and grace. I pray that my boys find confidence in all they do.

    Lord, I pray that K.S. seeks you in everything he does. I pray that his heart opens to reflect your kindness, compassion, and humility.

    In Your Name,
    Amen

Paranoia

It is against me
It lures me and debates me
It won't love me or relate to me
It hates me and wants to replace me
It tells me no one will ever embrace me
Because they will only hurt and break me
But make no mistake
The paranoia will not enslave me
As I see the lies it gave me

**Journal Entry
March 9, 2017**

Philippians 4:6-8
Stop worrying, pray more, focus on thoughts that are true, honorable, right and pure, lovely, and admirable. Think about things that are excellent and worthy of praise.

Psalm 139:24
Point out anything that offends you,
Dear Lord in heaven,

I pray to find patience in prayer and healing in your word. Am I following your will? Am I hearing your plan? Lord, I pray for a kind heart, confidence, and discernment.

Lord, I pray to focus more on understanding scripture and applying it to my life. Lord, I particularly pray for better self-control. Thank you for all the blessings you have bestowed upon me, Lord.

In your name,
Amen

Forgiveness

My Pastor says forgiveness is the word
To free us from all that is absurd
But the bonds of resentment and hatred are blurred
And keep me bound to the ways of the returned memories
And wickedness that never discerns
Between good and evil and all that I learned
But for the future and my sanity earned
I will forgive and let go as my pastor so urged
Revealing my hurt and learning to purge
That victim mentally so submerged
And replace it with God's peace
And all that I deserve
Once and for all I will emerge
Like a bold and beautiful wild free bird

Journal Entry
February 10, 2017

Pray for:
Sharp tongue
Negative attitude
Regular prayer
People to pray for:
My children
K.S.
Mr. Smith
(Silent prayer)
Feeling very distracted today, struggling to initiate prayer.

Even in darkness I cannot hide from you. To you the night shines as bright as the day. Darkness and light are the same to you" ****

I am in awe of your timing Lord.

Tricks

My mind plays tricks
Paranoia and hatred always affect
What my rational mind tries to protect, any sanity I have left
I apologize over and over to all I affect
I try so hard to stay above water
But the darkness drowns me, and I continue to be a bother
Insanity has a face like mine
Sending chills down my spine
The light stands firm in its might
Shining forever bright so I can see its plight
As it holds me in sight
But I will always, always continue the fight

Mindful Warrior

There is an ever-greater thread of spirituality that speaks to me. One that consistently remains emotionally present when the waves of my illness come and go. One that speaks to me from the wind through the trees, the waves of the ocean, the earthly dirt my feet are ground in, through an elemental force of divinity defined by the universe and Mother Nature.

It works in concert with all the universal elements—the moon, the sun, vibrational energies, and philosophical reasoning. Some might simply call it mindful awakening, in the presence of all that is nature and authenticity, akin to Buddhist and Hindu philosophies.

This is an email I received from a Christian in response to sufferers of mental illness:

Mental illness, in my opinion, is a crutch and a diluted excuse. Majority of mental illness is a satanic stronghold in society the Bible clearly states... Ephesians 6:12 "We wrestle not against flesh and blood, but the principalities of this earth" Does this mean Christians can't be mentally ill? NO, BUT if we could realize what kind of POWER, we have through the Holy Spirit we would not be mentally ill or need medication. Because our world doesn't know Christ, they don't know the deliverer of all sickness and the healer of our mind, body, and soul. They only like what they see and want to be medicated or taken care of instantly. Satan has blinded our eyes, confused society."

This email stirred me passionately. It's a reminder to me that if you pray and be the dutiful disciple, one person, one God, will cure you. As clear and present today is the very real mirroring of a vast majority of church followers: a false representation of the loving, humanitarian, forgiving, peaceful, and unjudging Jesus. This is not how I will find redemption, peace, and comfort from my monsters. Maybe if I pray enough, beg to the heavens enough, God or the universe will take this demonic incarceration from me. If only I'd been the good daughter my parents wanted and expected. Been the mother I should have been, the wife to my third husband I should have been, and the wife I need to be now. If I just met all the expectations, I'd be given a second chance. The reality of nature is I am my own savior.

I can't deny where my innate vibrational energies repeatedly took me, the elements where my mind found solace. Doug's wooded property. In the sand and waters of Orient, New York. The deep green forest of Sault Ste. Marie, Canada. And through the landscapes of Kenya. With nature comes this unapologetic, authentic, remarkable, bustling life. Whether created by a God or some other mystical forces, it doesn't come with a book. It speaks to you by evoking emotion.

The extraordinary properties of nature reflect minimalism, silent reflection, appreciation for its intricacies, and the ability to be truly mindful in each moment. It involves absorbing the positive energy from its underlying movements, expelling the negative from your soul, recycling it into its abundantly gracious scenery. Breathe it in; breathe it out. What philosophies like Buddhism stand to teach, so does nature. Let go of attachments and be mindful of your thoughts, while giving yourself time to rejuvenate your mind whether in meditation or simply breathing in the air on a long walk.

Mindfulness in War & Nature

Standing alone on a concrete slab
Everything around me is frozen
The chaos of the world in 360 degrees surrounds my body
Commencing to my left, screaming rioters blended into war
Tanks firing in desert conditions
Blurred into the human desire for material things
Trampling each other for the latest in technological
    advances
Aside the fearfully wild eyes of a sheep slaughtered, wool
    trenched in blood
Blended to vivid imagery of vast deforestation
Followed by the plastic-filled stomachs of marine souls
In a backdrop of a dying coral reef
Yet I feel embraced by a spiritual tranquility
My right hand wipes the images to nothingness, to only
    spiritual brilliance
The concrete dissipates and I am sublimely alone
Surrounded by the splendor of a glistening forest
Pure crisp air is welcomed by my heavy inhalation
Innately relaxed, unwary of my surroundings
Wildlife before me, virtuous, exuding merriment
I clearly glean the wind dancing through the leaves
I devour the subtle song of birds
Crickets chirping in harmony around me
I behold the intrinsic value of its divine beauty
Mother Nature's formation of flora is precise in liberating
    oxygen
With the rhythm of every working organism breathing life

I'M NOT AFRAID OF THE MONSTERS

A break in my reticular activation system, my brain's
    gatekeeper
To be extraordinarily and consciously aware of it all
I run my fingers over the green moss of the old oak tree
Its pulse is my pulse
And together we are free

SIXTEEN

In the Now

My husband is a fixer to a fault. Since day one he stepped up, looking my darkness in the face, taking it on at my side. As if my battle would always be his battle too. Even pushing the limits of his emotional health, he tries to talk through every situation to the tenth degree. It genuinely plagues him that he can't fix me. Instead, he strives to make me happy by always saying or doing the right thing. He aims to make me laugh and smile and buys me thoughtful little gifts, in hopes everything will be good.

Just a few short hours into his patrol shift he was called to our own home regarding a violent act I committed. Arriving in a state of shock and confusion, he threw himself to his knees before me, placing my hands in his, looking up to me with a *where did it all go wrong* look.

In Southern martyr fashion, he doesn't contemplate why I did what I did that day with his Glock, initially. Rather, he questions why his actions weren't enough. Questioning how he could patrol the streets day in and day out, seeing similar illness and scenarios, yet missing the signs at home. As I look down at him in that moment, he is visibly afraid. He is afraid of what I am capable of, afraid of what my illness is capable of.

Arriving at this state, this day, was months of grooming at the hands of my monsters. I was Initially fed a mental high with resolute egocentric thinking. I was a plant-based beacon of health. I didn't want anything toxic in my body. Whispers said I should quit the medication I had been taking to move to an optimal all-natural health approach. Furthermore, because this lifestyle would lead me to prime mental health, I thus didn't need them. I was confident in my decision, but not confident enough to tell anyone else. My monsters are skillful when they strike. Boosted ego, limitless energy, and increased creativity.

Always predictable, each high is chased by a low. Intense self-doubt brought on by accusations, ulterior motives to sabotage me, and distrust of friends and family. I had constant chatter in my head regarding all my shortcomings day in and day out. My brain was in a constant whirlwind of fight or flight mode carried by a tornado of that bipolar mixed state. Bipolar depression and mania colliding forcefully, each trying to vie for dominance over the other, adding an atmosphere of agitation.

To my husband, this can appear something like inconsistent and irrational arguments, verbal assaults, anger, with fits of laughter, crying, or hypersexual or hyposexual behavior. Yet he missed the signs because he internalized my assaults, honestly believing I was attacking his inadequacies. Making it about him, taking on all the responsibility. Even in law enforcement, he was no match for my darkness. It's cunning, unpredictable, and knows no boundaries. As I chase its whispers, unmedicated, suffering the fate of two dominant forces in my brain, I was about to ignite.

Journal Entry
May 21, 2017

    An underlying presence of paranoia, negative self-talk, and insecurities is present. They speak to me quietly but creep in like early morning fog taking over my mind throughout the day. The uncomfortable noise amidst my silence builds like a pressure cooker. By midday I can hardly focus on simple tasks as I overthink and overanalyze my shortcomings.

    Today is a church day. I enter in with a smile on my face despite my hesitation to even enter the building where I am greeted with your typical pleasantries and today's sermon outline. I walk to my usual section of seating. I am a creature of habit in this regard, some seven rows back, middle section, last seats on the left. I whisper to God, "Lord, please help me focus on today's message. Please allow me to hear you over all my distractions." Our pastor has suggested that when you are married, more difficulties will bestow upon you as Satan will work harder to break the covenant you entered into. It's been three weeks since Pastor Ralph officiated our marriage before God and our family.

    Today, I pick a fight. It's like I have no control, like the devil himself has taken over my mouth and I am unable to stop myself. Despite what I have learned I initially lack the ability to reflect patience, grace, or love in this moment. As does my dear husband.

I retreat to the porch to clear my head. Dearest husband comes to me before he leaves for work. "What is wrong dear?" I hang my head as to not make eye contact. He grabs my face, lifts me to his, and says, "Look at me, the husband who loves you, the man you can trust and confide in, the man who will always be here for you." I sink into his arms, and I cry. I realize the dark season is returning; it's progressive like a cancer. How long before the monster reappears? Will I be better armed with prayer and Christ in my newfound salvation? Will I successfully combat the terror in my head while studying the bible?

There is a quote by author Martha Manning in her book *Undercurrents*. "Depression is such a cruel punishment. There are no fevers, no rashes, no blood tests to send people scurrying in concern, just the slow erosion of self, as insidious as cancer. And like cancer, it is essentially a solitary experience: a room in hell with only your name on the door."

But it is this scripture I will repeat to find solace, Isaiah 41:10 "...do not fear, for I am with you, do not be afraid, for I am your God; I will strengthen you, I will help you, I will uphold you with my victorious right hand."

Journal Entry
November 18, 2018

Me: (Text) I feel like shit.

Husband: (Text) Get some rest

Me: (Text) I don't want to fucking rest. My head is scaring me. DELETE, DELETE, DELETE. My head is angry, I will probably take Tylenol PM, drink a beer, and think about stabbing myself in the neck. DELETE, DELETE, DELETE, DELETE.

Me: (Actually Text) Okay

Who do I have to talk about this fucked up shit in my head? About how I fell to the floor hyperventilating in a sudden bout of hysterics? Who do I talk to when I feel like slicing my arm just to feel the pain? No one understands. They probably think I'm dramatic, ridiculous, or attention-seeking. They have no clue. My mind is off. Laughing one minute, crying uncontrollably the next followed by visions of stabbing myself.

Tranquility

Even the darkness is quiet here
Submerged in water up over my ear
Nothing but the echoing of my own heart beating
The water is a forcefield to everything mistreating
I keep in time with my breaths
So I can forget all the rest
All my sensitivities dissipate
I'll never want to leave at this rate
This is a safe place, there is no fear
For even the darkness is quiet here

Journal Entry
March 23, 2019

Day 3 or 4 of no meds. No use of antidepressants. Aside from being slightly more sensitive, I haven't noticed any symptoms. It is the beginning of Spring, the sun is out so naturally I am feeling better, have more energy, and happier. This might also be because I am leaving another job that makes me very unhappy.

Journal Entry
April 16, 2019

It's all coming back to me in flashes. You came back. I haven't felt you in a while. You're always there, I need to wake up.

Journal Entry
November 6, 2019

Physical changes:
Weight up, Face shape fuller

Emotional:

Hysterical laughing followed by significant fatigue.

Cold distance followed by neediness then paranoia

SEVENTEEN

Secure Room One

"Mrs. Stieh, what's your goal for the day?" Barely awake, confused by the question, and harboring agitation for being there, I snapped, "What?!" Sensing my mood, the flamboyant, entirely too front and center for the day, young medical technician sensed my disposition, and without skipping a beat he slowly mocked me: "Whaaat isss yoour goalll forrr too-daay?" *Oh, we're doing this, buddy. I am having no part in this banter.* I wanted to say that my goal for today was to find the quickest way to get the fuck out of this place. He stood there, one hand on hip, the other holding his pen in a hover over his clipboard and paper, waiting impatiently to write down my response and then move on. "I have no idea!" I insisted. Almost as quickly as the words bounced off my lips, his eyes rolled, and his toe tapped in unison with a tongue click. "To be positive maybe?" I fully anticipated that to be followed with, geez lady, did you forget where you are? Begrudgingly I muttered, "Sure, that's exactly right."

Secure room one was my temporary home in the psychiatric facility that I now found myself. It typically hosted those who might be a threat to themselves or others. It was from what I could see the only private, single-bed room with a camera monitor, a small bathroom, and a second reinforced door adorned with an intimidating steel locking mechanism affixed to the outside. It looks slightly like a bank vault. Keeps anyone inside from getting out. After a couple of bed moves in the first twenty-four hours, I quickly earned myself these accommodations after one volatile dining hall encounter.

Another grossly upbeat technician, Louie, a red-headed, young, stocky guy with a verbally expressed fan crush on Brittany Spears, directed everyone to the dining hall for lunch and vitals. "Line up over here for vitals when you finish eating and put away your tray!" he announced across an already loud and bustling room. I took in all the faces, all the cross conversations echoing throughout the hall, a mounted sixty-five-inch television blaring the most popular pop songs, while the *tap, tap, tap, tap* of the paddles hitting that little plastic ball off the ping-pong table. An intense anxiousness rose from my chest, adding a pronounced rapid heartbeat. A fierce radiating heat moved up through my shoulders, up into my neck, my face, out my pores, ears, and eyes. My left-hand fingers twitched as my hyperawareness was more than I could bear.

I frantically braced myself, gripping the plastic arms of my chair, then slamming my hands over my ears, then back and forth between the two as I was trying to quiet my head and support my now off-kilter body. Louie spotted me in my current condition. "Rivka, why don't you come get your vitals done now?" Not hesitating on that request, I leapt from my chair rapidly, making it from point A to point B, some eight feet between us. Leo gently and politely acknowledged my distress and instructed me softly on what to do next. "Put the oxygen monitor on your right ring finger," he said as he wrapped the blood pressure cuff tightly around my left arm. The cuff uncomfortably gripped my skin. In my hypersensitive state, my insides felt as if they were banging on my skin to escape. I could barely remain still. The music was painful to my ears now, and someone tapped their chair to its beat, amplifying the strains. I screamed, "Get me out of here!" Leo yanked the cuff and monitors off my arm while pointing directly to the hall. "Go ahead…" His words trailed off as I rushed out the double doors, one propped open by a chair I tried not to trip over.

A nurse walking by, holding someone else's medications in a little white cup, stopped me by placing one hand on my shoulder, grounding me. I suddenly couldn't speak and madly paced back and forth. "What's the matter, dear?" Everyone here seemed genuinely concerned about my well-being. And for all the patients. In my first night I shared a room with an elderly woman, Laura, also restless and unable to sleep. She was thin, frail, her long gray hair laid on the shoulder of her white nightgown with blue flowers.

She stood in the doorway, the glow of the hall light on her face. She was communicating with unintelligible words, to herself, to me, to anyone who would walk by. An older nurse, both gentle in her touch and words, gained my roommate's trust and guided her back to bed. The nurse comforted her. "Okay, dear, let's lay down and get you back to sleep." Then this kind, sweet-tempered nurse did something that changed even my apprehension in this place. She said, "Laura, would it be okay if I pray with you?" Laura only responded with a murmur, but the nurse proceeded. "Dear Lord, please comfort Laura and wrap her in your love so she may sleep peacefully. Fight her battles, dear Lord, lift her out from fear. Lord, help her spirit wake rested and with faith in your mercy. In Jesus' name, Amen."

In my current fear, I looked to the nurse who stopped me in the hall. "I…I…I…don't know, so much noise…I…I…can't breathe, I can't breathe," I breathlessly stuttered while hyperventilating. I couldn't remain still through an eruption of sobs. "I don't know what's wrong with me!"

"It's going to be okay. Just take this and some deep breaths." Her voice was comforting. Another nurse joined in with a new little white cup, with one little white pill inside, just for me. No better way than to stop an incoherent, sobbing psychiatric patient than Ativan, a cup of water, and words of endearment.

This is how you get a free upgrade to secure room one. Devon, the night supervisor, tall, engaging, articulate, and handsome, pulled me aside. "Rivka, we're going to put you in another room. You're going to like this one. It's quiet and at the end of the hall." Devon was another nurse who spoke with a genuine responsibility to the patients. Pointing to the room, handing me my few items, he told me to get settled in. "We'll be heading to dinner soon."

To be honest, I did like secure room one. It was small and to some may have seemed too confined. To me, was exactly as its name implied, secure. Which signifies safety, restful, and quiet. It was a solitary room for reflection. It encouraged comfort and compliance. I picked up a book, *Before We Were Yours*. I became engulfed in the tale of Queenie and her siblings, a period piece, based on a true story of white poor children being kidnapped and adopted out to rich white families. That book and the brown journals I was given to write kept me from obsessing over what I did to get here.

I don't want to romanticize my stay. Psychiatric wards are full of commotion and oftentimes hysteria. During a call with my oldest daughter, on a communal phone in a short hallway, one middle-aged woman with evident around-the-clock needs began a violent tirade, rushing and flexing as if to hit staff. While everyone else was running to the nearest room I was trapped right in the middle, in direct contact with her. And she certainly looked to be aware I was there. My daughter's voice was distinctly sad and distraught for the circumstances and the event taking place. I tried not to cry, attempting to speak as if nothing was happening, commotion ensuing behind me. It was upsetting to my daughter and scary for me.

The psych ward was full of sad and angry people. If you're like me, an empath so to speak, I find it hard to not take on the mood of a room. One more positive to secure room one was that it isolated me from all that emotion. But you could hear every word from the hallway. Not all the nurses were genuine. Two familiar voices approached outside, which also happened to be beside the elevator. One Ukrainian nurse and another young nurse I'd seen around were talking together, disgruntled. "Are you telling me you're going to believe the word of some psychotic asshole over me?" She was repeating a conversation she apparently had with a supervisor earlier.

On a more personal level, I experienced sedating or downright debilitating reactions to new medications. The right drug for someone with mental illness is really a crapshoot. If you want to get better, you do what it takes to get there, and that means multiple medication attempts until you hit the jackpot with the right little pill or even a combination thereof.

I had reactions to medications so extreme that I cried and begged nurses for sedatives so I could sleep until the effects wore off. One made my entire body feel like it was experiencing restless leg syndrome, only in every limb and every part of my body. Add in an overall outrageous feeling of uneasiness so severe that I couldn't sit, speak well, or control my emotions. My husband, who dutifully came to see me every night, experienced this firsthand when I immediately left him standing in the visitors' room, abruptly rushing back to my bed, rocking back and forth neurotically.

My medication lottery was pulled when I met my new psychiatrist, post-hospitalization, when he prescribed a combination of Lithium and Wellbutrin. One was a mood stabilizer and the other an antidepressant to provide extra support warding off depressive states. Later adding Lamictal for extra support of anger. This doctor was also the first to enforce compliance, holding me accountable. "Look, if you don't take these pills, you're going to end up killing someone or killing yourself." No one had ever expressed the severity of my illness like that. He went on to explain the subtle link between bipolar and schizophrenia, how they affect the same area of the brain. Then he gave me the odds that I would end up back in the hospital based on statistical data he stored in his psychiatrist's mind. He claimed a bipolar patient typically experiences one major episode that warrants hospitalization every three years. He was frank and informative. No passive attempts in discussing the significance of my illness with him.

I spent five full days in this psychiatric retreat, attending all the pertinent activities. The patients who arrived before me explained how to walk the line for a quick departure: Attend all the groups, meet with the psychologist and psychiatrist, and I should be out by the end of the week. It can take you aback how fast you begin to genuinely create some empathy for the people who share so much of themselves in such a short period of time. Each one has a unique environmental contributing factor with underlying mental illness bringing them to this hospital, in this ward. With not so unique a diagnosis. Major depression, anxiety disorders, obsessive-compulsive disorder, post-traumatic stress disorder, and bipolar disorder seemed to top the list. Many carried the burden of multiple diagnoses, as well as a lengthy history of numerous doctors, a barrage of medications, varying therapies, and little in the way of family support. Furthermore, like me, they could recall experiencing their ailments for as long as they could remember.

The other patients, primarily younger than me, eighteen to twenty-five, possibly felt comfortable opening up to me as a mother figure. I was in my forties, quite older, though I didn't quite meet the same needs or illnesses as those in the older ward. An adjoining hallway included mostly patients forty and up. They were like my first roommate, rather catatonic, incontinent, hysterical, and otherwise combative.

There was Arthur, a young, awkward boy who had a traumatic brain injury from a car accident that affected his frontal lobe and essentially his behavior and impulses. Abby, a quiet, shy, grief-stricken girl with long, mousy hair had lost a baby. Her depression scared even herself with increasing suicidal ideation. Aaron, he was thin and wiry, wore BCG-type eyeglasses. The kind they give you in the Army with thick black frames and large lenses. BCG is named for their appearance. Birth control glasses. Aaron wore a flattop haircut also similar to someone in the military. He had not served, but he suffered long-term post-traumatic stress disorder, had multiple personalities, suffered from child abuse, and recently tried to hang himself.

Chris was an academic type, extremely articulate, well read, educated, blond ponytail, who tried to kill his father for raping him as a child. Another, I can't recall his name, but I always referred to his appearance. Frat boy. He overindulged in prescription drugs and alcohol. Ethan was a tall and very sturdily built American Indian with shoulder-length brown hair. He rarely spoke, the epitome of the strong, silent type. What little I gathered had a lot to do with family upheaval and alcoholism. Echo, a beautiful young woman, a lesbian, faced discrimination from her family and unexplained, long-term depression. Dan, a constantly smiling young kid, had overdosed on a prescription of Ativan. And Lauren, a heavyset, dark-haired, mostly silent girl with unpredictable behavior, also suffered from a TBI, traumatic brain injury.

Initially I couldn't bring myself to speak to them. I sat back and observed. It took me a few days to even acknowledge anyone let alone make eye contact. But I was paying attention to everything. Day four, just forty-eight hours from my discharge, I felt open. The agitation was gone, the hypersensitivity had dissipated, and I actually felt good. To my own surprise I was talkative.

"Hi, Lauren, how are you?"

Lauren: "Good morning."

Chris, a very chatty fellow in general, saw my sudden brightness. "Good morning looks like you're feeling good. Nice to see you talking to us today."

My new positive demeanor made the classes more bearable, and actually a little fun. How could I continue to be so morose when these kids, who had experienced some really terrible things, could exchange idle chitchat, even smile and laugh?

It seemed that everyone prior to their discharge met with a psychiatrist who conducted a lengthy test to determine the most accurate diagnosis based on their responses. Although I had been informally diagnosed with bipolar disorder in the past, that didn't seem concrete or real to me. This testing, I hoped, would not only adequately provide the best diagnosis but also pinpoint the level of bipolar disorder I identified. If in fact, I am bipolar. Bipolar is categorized by two levels based on severity. Bipolar I am defined by severe mood episodes from mania to depression. Bipolar II is defined as milder hypomania alternating with periods of depression.

When it was my turn, and the results came back, I actually felt a sudden bout of despair. Although this had been my life for years, it was now official in some way. With the diagnosis of bipolar disorder, type I, I felt life-sentenced to my monsters. I am bipolar with aggressive tendencies and a hint of addictive traits with an identified overindulgence to alcohol. I can't deny this discovery. Two defining violent incidents in my life and one DUI after consuming too much Red Bull and vodka could support those findings.

The aggression, that's the real monster. My doctors have reason to be concerned for the submerged storm I carry. I've felt angry since my pre-adolescent years, and it never left. Stress hormones replaced the serotonin, creating optimal conditions for a walking, raging teenager. I could become easily hostile, provoked or unprovoked. Manufacturing someone capable of violence, emotionally devastating, a victimizer. Someone capable of the charge, in concert with an assault with a deadly weapon. Remanded to the custody of their parents at fifteen years old, with supervised probation until the age of eighteen.

I wasn't without remorse. Occasionally my psychological disconnect would clear. After all, I had turned myself in and accepted my restitution. The real restitution, a life sentence of nightmares and unrelenting shame that I wear like a thick wool sweater. Itchy and abrasive to my skin. A reminder of the victims' faces. Unable to articulate my heinous actions, I create the pretense of a drug problem, seeking some kind of help. To which I was committed to a mental health facility for the first time under the false pretense of addiction.

Following this inpatient stay, dependent on several factors, I would be placed in Intensive Outpatient Treatment, which is a full-day classroom group therapy. Weaning down to a partial day program acclimating you back into the real world. Or go straight to the partial program. Given my circumstances, the first was apparent. With really no other choice, I attend. I unequivocally did not want a repeat of what I had just experienced over the previous seven days. My eyes and mind were now wide open to the recommendations of the therapists and psychologists running the program. It led me to my new psychiatrist, beginning an entirely new journey. A life-defining, make-it or break-it moment.

Darkness

The darkness is a vice inside my head
It never leaves and talks to me with dread
Whispering and manipulating every word said
Despite the fight, I cannot seem to ace
This darkness in its wicked place
I try to shake this cold dead space
A little white pill has been my only saving grace
From this dark and wicked place

Inpatient and outpatient experiences are vastly different when compared to generalized therapy. Inpatient was, for me, an introduction to terms like radical acceptance, self-care, and mindfulness. And an immersive outpatient therapy program is where it gets raw, painful, and reflective. I loved it and hated it. Initially excited to get in my car and whisk to the group, I also sat in my car debating on actually attending, frozen.

This type of therapy puts into motion a real emotional and spiritual experience. It reminded me that journaling was always a great way to reflect and gauge my illness. It's not only cathartic, but no matter how crazy my thoughts seemed on paper, I could track my monster, create a timeline of events, and monitor triggers. In the pages of my journal, I could see more clearly how my bipolar pendulum controlled me, while intensive therapy armed me with the encouragement to accept and manage it. I was willing to put in the work to see that happen.

When I really began to feel comfortable in my own skin expressing real and raw emotions, I needed to say my crime. I needed to say what I had done out loud. Not only to get it off my chest but maybe even slightly expecting someone's disdain for my actions, earning me some damnation. I wanted to be punished for my actions, even though I was punishing myself enough on my own. And even though I have come to know I can extend myself a level of grace for my pre-medicated, monster-driven, past self.

Let me set this stage for you. I am a liberal, humanitarian, vegan, animal activist, planet activist, cop's wife, mother of four, and senator's daughter from a city-like suburban lifestyle. Unlike the country conditions, in which I now reside. As a vegan, I keep a ninety-five percent vegan household, only allowing non-plant-based items when my son comes home for college, we entertain other people who bring their own food, or when my youngest daughter brings home dino nuggets or pizza rolls.

Having that been said, I reside in a rural community where we are surrounded by cattle farmers to every side. So close in fact that I dread leaving the house on days the farmers rip the babies from their mothers. Hearing the mothers cry out with grief all day. Hell, I even cry when I pass the empty pig transports because when it's empty that means a load of intelligent sentient beings has already been slaughtered. Which makes my crime even harder to express.

On the dreaded day, I sat at the end of my bed, determined to pick up a particular gun, the one with no safety. In my disconnected state, like an out-of-body experience, I stepped outside and took note of my surroundings. It was a sunny and clear April day with a blue sky and slight wind. Two adult potbelly pigs and three babies had gotten out and were foraging the grass nearby. This wasn't unusual; they get out a lot. I separated the babies by tossing some grain in the opposite direction while corralling the two adults back into the pen. Both females. The largest, a mother, was often combative. Charging you like a battle ram, biting and nipping at your legs, and snarling with what seemed rageful discontent. She had begun to terrorize the smaller female, about half her size, occasionally biting on her own babies, one bearing more of the brunt, losing hair, and much thinner than her siblings.

At that moment, standing there, still emotionless, a movie reel of all that compounded the anger in my head and chest was surfacing. This deep-rooted feeling of agitation went beyond simple annoyance. It was fury. I was aware of it, but not feeling it. Like someone with schizophrenia, it's as if a version of me who wasn't affected by emotions came forward to protect me, to handle the situation. That altered self-raised the gun, pointing it directly at the bully. The one who represented everything that made me angry at this moment, and I shot her. Not just once or twice. Repeatedly. I couldn't stop, one bullet after another until the magazine was either empty or close to it. The other pig looked on in horror and panic, pacing the fence line the farthest from me. I just committed the unthinkable. I just gruesomely murdered a pig who was simply experiencing a little post-partum aggression and needed to be spayed. She had been entrusted to me, to care for her, love her, and ensure her safety. I'm a killer.

Every animal rights group can shame me, chastise me. I deserve it. But this is what mental illness, monsters, darkness, does to you. It turns you into someone you don't recognize. Someone you loathe, you are ashamed of, pray will disappear, sometimes even wish were dead. Bipolar disorder takes you whole, shakes you up, tears apart the important pieces of you and then leaves you jumbled and out of sorts. You'll never get the puzzle of you back together. You will always be the puzzle with that one missing piece you can never find.

Journal Entry
March 12, 2020

    I have got to get it together.

    I am spinning out of control. Work, home, food, etc. I am trying to recall my coping skills and unplug from the things that are creating chaos and anxiety. So many things causing continually exacerbated negativity, even on social media. I need to regrasp that peace and quietness my heart needs.

Journal Entry
March 18, 2020

The vision.

I was driving to work while listening to the tranquility of yoga mantra vibrational music to begin my day with peace going into the toxic environment of my employment. I'm relaxed, initially aware of my driving. At some point I become so entranced by the music it takes over my body and a vivid scene appears in my mind.

I'm facing my darkness, my upside down but I am not feeling afraid. I feel and see from my peripheral there is light to my back. I turn to face it and see a tree with umbrella like branches. It is similar or is the Bodhi tree. Underneath the branches of the tree is a man. He sits like a Buddhist monk in a meditation pose. I feel calm and think to myself, why am I here. Then the yogi looks up and I follow his gaze. The sky above is flickering between day and night showing me a crescent moon and awaken.

I made it to work but recall very little of my drive. I researched what it means to envision the yogi and a crescent moon. It's indicative of following a path and spiritual awakening. I know what I have been feeling is right. There must be more. I can awaken another part of me to be a better conduit of God's light and energy, as well as that of the universe.

Journal Entry
April 5, 2020

This past week has been strange in retrospect. I was neither joyful nor angry. I was simply being. Although I participated in meaningless gossip at work there was no emotion attached to it. I remained positive, outgoing, and polite. I am returning to the job I had prior as it made me feel good and encouraged in my role there.

I completed 10 minutes of guided meditation. I need to start listing to those that resonate with me.

Poetry Thought*

Let flowers bloom in my open wounds. Making roots like spreading ivy filling in all the old dead spaces. Giving me new life it demands oxygen and light as it grounds my feet to Mother Nature. I am now one with earth and earth one with me. My soul now aligned with her energy.

The darkness is supressed.

Journal Entry
April 7, 2020

It's been an evening full of unnecessary overindulgence of food and wine. My night restless and amplified by an overwhelming sense of uncomfortableness, anxiety, and hot flashes before waking quite early.

I step outside onto our front porch, first mindful of the symphony of croaks, chirps, clucks, and ribbits from the new frogs of spring. Our barn cats lazily strung about. I take deep breaths in of the morning fresh air, then look up. The dark sky is filled with a powerful glow, and I'm intrigued by how extraordinarily bright it seems.

There it is, the culprit to my insanity, the imbalance to my physical self, and the gravitational pull to my mental instability. Yet this super moon, a pink moon, draws me in. Her magnetism is intoxicating. When she is bright and full she demands an audience, and an audience she gets. I can't help being drawn to her beauty, her radiant energy, need her. I soak her up like a crystal rejuvenating its healing properties under her magnificent show.

She is so powerful, lunatic quite literally comes from the word lunar. Many Buddhist monasteries believe in the moon's effect on all living things and encourage spending full moon days and nights at home in spiritual development. Enhancing skills to enlightenment to concentrate this time on peace and happiness to calm the senses.

Journal Entry
April 8, 2020

It's eighty degrees today. What spring brings.

Her rays flow through my retinas seducing hormones in my brain. My serotonin levels rise. She interrupts my circadian rhythm, influencing changes to my metabolism and energy. The universe and spring are connected. The veil of darkness lifts and I see them. The noise in my head subsides. I must shed everything that holds me back. Shed everything that interferes with my spiritual growth, creativity, and intended life path.

I quit another meaningless, mundane, and toxic job. I yearn for higher learning. I can't get enough of subjects that all intertwine into one common path. Enlightenment, ahimsa, Ram Dass, Yogananda, reiki, feng shui, astrology, Ayurveda, spirit animals, intuitiveness, HSP (highly sensitive people), Buddhism, and the Dali Lama.

I know this drive all too well. I feel like a mad scientist. My creativity soars. I have rapid thoughts and an increased need to talk. And a constant drive to know why, understand more, have all the answers. I need to know the meaning of my existence. I research relentlessly. Sudtelties from the universe lead me from one direction to the next.

I read, watch documentaries, try to sleep through guided meditations, and exuberantly commit to affirmations. I buy everything and anything that will help me commit to my new journey. Yoga mats, gold fish (eight colored and one black per feng shui tradition), clothes, Buddha statue, books and more books, singing bowls, sage sticks, and a plethora of online courses.

My mind never shuts down. I indulge a little more in alcohol to take the edge off. Sleep less to cram in more daylight. And focus on my goal.

Journal Entry
April 9, 2020

I am the cause of all my own suffering. If I cannot control negative external factors, then I must be the root cause of all my suffering. *Eats cookie batter contemplating this thought.

I eat feverishly mixing up, stirring about, taking a bite of this and that, from one item to the next swirling around the kitchen. No cognizant thought about the food, the eating, just me doing. I have managed to eat leftovers, cookie dough, and crackers before I race to my room for TV and relaxation. I am suddenly aware of my fast movements and rapid chewing atop the fullness of my stomach.

What was I doing, why was I doing it, how was I so unconscious of my binging state? More importantly, if I am the root cause of all my suffering, the suffering is me, then I am my darkness. I am my monster; I am the devil on my back. My bipolar disorder is a part of me, and I am a part of it.

Journal Entry
April 14, 2020

Guided Meditation, PTSD

I follow the voice as I sit still on my pillow. It begins, allow the painful memories to come to you, the ones you want to heal from. My memories were laid before me like a deck of playing cards. I see my ten-year-old self sitting cross-legged on the floor of my old fifth grade elementary school pod. She says nothing, but I know she is full of shame and guilt. I see from her the boys who taunted us that have no idea what we experienced at home.

I kneel to her; I stroke her face moving her hair from her forehead. The guided voice was to forgive those who hurt us and ourselves. I look to her and stand with her hand in mine. "We are forgiven, we can forgive ourselves." I look to my young self, "It's not your fault." And I let her go. This is the hardest part, saying goodbye to myself, I didn't want to let her go. She waved to me, and I waved goodbye, "It's going to be okay."

I sift through the memory cards that lead in chronological order all the way to this past weekend. I forgive them. I forgive myself. I'm to heal my wounds now and close them up. A white light begins circling my brain, my heart, my lower abdomen, and my eyes as if it's washing them. I am suddenly emotional as I see small

and large wounds closing up all over my body.
The light is cauterizing them.

Journal Entry
April 18, 2020

I'm not always unaware or in any kind of trance state to have a very vivid meditation experience. Or hallucination. Today I lit a candle and incense then performed a few prostrations. Then with meditation music began a journey.

I'm walking through a dense forest with a rushing creek beside me. I was enjoying it. The feeling of the sun on my face between the leaves, the earthy smells, the feel of the dirt on my barefoot toes, and the vivid hues of blues and greens.

As I walk, I speak a mantra, "I am courageous, I am strong, I am smart, I am loving kindness, I am loving awareness." The forest suddenly opened to a flat plain and I continued, "I am strong, I am courageous, I am loving kindness." It felt good to yell it loudly,

I continue repeating the mantra when the plain opens to an ocean full of waves and it's dark. There's no sunlight. I walk completely into the water and submerge. I am looking at myself in front of me. I tell her, "It's okay to let go, just let it go." I watch myself take in the water and choke then twitching a bit until she falls to the ocean floor. I look face to face with her, her eyes are closed there's no sign of life.

Another new me emerges from the ocean floor to a warm and sunny sandy beach. It's ten-year-old me, she is screaming with veracity and rage, "I am strong, I am courageous, I am loving kindness!" An ethereal hand grabs the hand of my ten-year-old self walking her toward a bright white light. The angel like being is telling her "Everything is going to be okay." The feminine presence kneels to her, touches her face, "You're going to be just fine, you are strong and courageous, you are loving kindness." Then she lets her go and remains in its place. My young self looks to me, then to the light and anxiously runs through the light.

Journal entry
April 22nd, 2020

I am with it all — Mindfulness Walking
I am with the grass under my feet
I am with every fallen branch, every leaf on the trees
Every old stump with character, every sapling
I am with every dandelion and little violet flower
I am with the vast gray sky. I am with the clouds
I am with everything that represents the history around me
I am with the old, barbed wire
I am with every post
I am with the sound of the birds calling and the frogs chirping
I am with the sound of the little bug buzzing by my ear
I am with the mud and grass clippings
I am with the little creek bed to the North
I am with the old broken cellar door
I am with all that represents the new
I am with the here and the now

Journal Entry
July 27th, 2020

Aging
Let my skin tell the story
My wrinkles will tell you of all the glory days
So many ups and downs, you can see them in my frown
Just let my eyes speak for themselves
Aging comes with fear my dear
Family and friends start dying, your kids grow and stop replying
But a new normal can be dignifying
Let my skin tell the story
Finding a new hobby and focusing on my body
Realizing all that's important
Family and friends, all those good memories
Let my skin tell the story
That I am taking a mental inventory
Every wrinkle, spot, line and by God's design
The story will be how humble and freeing age can really be

Journal Entry
August 1st, 2020

    Clanging — the condition of rhyming in mental health disorders
    Poetic words flow freely in my head
    Trying to sleep to no avail
    I just want to rhyme down this long and winding trail
    It never ends this poetic imagery
    Filling my mind so I'll see
    How fabulous the colors and textures can be
    I can't stop so I write and write trying to set them free

Journal Entry
August 2, 2020

Narcissist

Do you even know who you are? Because it really seems so far. It's removed from my memory. Were you ever really there for me? You have me so confused now. Maybe I should take a bow. For your skillful performance.

EIGHTEEN

The After

I never felt in writing this book there was ever a, The End, only a The After. Your illness never ends with an archetypal happily ever after, but rather a pivotal moment in which your world is turned upside down and clarity surfaces in order for an awakening to take place. My alternate universe, the monster with no distinguishable features, the darkness looming with the promise of death, and the battle of my conscious and subconscious mind in silent communication of intuitive tugs to save my life are no longer.

Everything seems lighter, clearer, and promising. I'm armed now, armed with awareness. Armed with the knowledge that I have successfully adequate resources and the skills to implement new coping skills. Being cognizant of mood shifts has a tremendous impact on their severity. Simply being so in tune to a manic state or depression is truly remarkable. You can't stop it, but you can ride it out with a different perspective.

Example: having a manic episode in which I couldn't sleep for seventy-two hours while I sketched out my future home to scale, obsessing over each detail. To describe my awareness in that moment is almost surreal. It's sitting on the sideline observing. It's reminding myself that this is temporary. It's an armchair coach, ensuring my safety, and keeping me in line.

Agitation, paranoia, melancholy is a bit trickier. I'm present, but there is a greater distinction in the impact I have on its outcome. My intuitive nature is weaker and unsteady. The emotions are more invasive like a quickly spreading disease. Getting ahead of it is nearly impossible. It's simply present; in some manner of unrest you are now able to recognize it for what it is, irrational. The difference is, you've acknowledged it but remain somewhat powerless to its stronghold on your brain. I grasp to some reality while reminding myself of its impermanence.

As a more stable medicated woman, I am grateful for how considerably more positive I am when each episode comes to an end. It's liberating in a healthy way. My life feels less dire. I count more good days than bad. Each altercation to my psyche is shorter in duration and leaves little to no scars. If I feel the burden becoming more grand, I discuss it with my doctor, who can determine if a prescription change may be warranted. There is always a way to remain steadfastly in control. I simply must not fight it, working against myself. I cannot and will not allow my monsters to win. Not again, not ever.

NINTEEN

Family & Friends

The awakening is yours and yours alone. There are so many variables to your success, and it can be just as complicated as in The Before. If you are married, have troubled relationships with family members and friends, or have been in trouble with the law, your success doesn't have as much of an impact if you haven't paid restitution. In more ways than one.

You have to come to terms with the fact that not everyone will accept a new you. In fact, you may even be held to a higher standard, an unrealistic expectation out of resentment. They will criticize your current behavior as illogical, flawed, deceitful, an imposter, or even arrogant. If they can't move on, how dare you for moving forward. They don't want to believe or admit there could be a better image of you as long as they're still hurt and angry. And we have to accept that.

I don't hold unrealistic expectations for the comprehension of my illness by friends and family. I let them come to their own level of understanding in their own time. And as long as they remain in my life,

I am graced with their loyalty and ability to separate me as a human being from my illness. I cherish those relationships with family and friends no matter how infrequent I may seem them. Friendships are valued at a level never before.

It's emotionally trying when it's people you love keeping you at arm's length. Ruminating becomes sadness and hours of tears, begging, and pleading for some shared empathy. Nothing I can do will expedite their healing. I can apologize, say I understand, and give them the space they need, and that too can cause descension. This growth of understanding has to happen organically. If it ever happens.

I believe there is something in the addict's twelve-step process regarding making amends and accepting the consequences. For me, the hardest part was being so out of touch to think everyone was past it already. That they saw my growth and appreciated it or even admired it. I was very wrong. They don't understand the battle. And they don't have to. Children didn't ask to be brought into your nightmare. Parents spend countless nights and days sick with worry, so much so your illness affected their life as much as it does yours. And all of the sudden you're just better? When growth should be a moment of rejoicing, it's resentment.

Be courageous and strong. Hold steady with your love and grace toward them. No matter the outcome, do not give up your resolve to show your commitment to a resolution. Don't hold on to them in the past. Just continue proving every day where you are now and who you have become through your actions. Recognize that in some cases, continuing a relationship with someone will only hinder your growth and stability. And be okay with that.

Here I am. This is me, past and all. I no longer apologize, because it only holds me back. And I refuse to take any steps in that direction. I allow myself sadness for what was. Good and the bad. I've accepted how my life has considerably shifted, leaving some of me behind. I have mourned the loss of parts of me I enjoyed and made people smile while manic. I grieved the loss of my old identity. I am celebrating every day in a big or small way that I am alive. That I am here to tell my story. I am unashamed and open about my history in order to potentially save another person. Accept me as I am, or don't and step aside.

To all my friends, past & present,

What it really means when I don't accept your invite. It means my brain is too tired to exert the energy required to fake a smile, make idle chitchat, or hold conversations. It means my body physically doesn't want to work in order to go anywhere or do anything. Sometimes, mental exhaustion even causes physical symptoms. Headaches, stomachaches, muscle aches, exacerbated PMS, and more.

It means I am trying out a new medication and I have no idea how it will affect me in the real world, and I am feeling a little uncomfortable already. It means, I can't drink with my medications, and I don't want to be that person that everyone says, "Oh, you're not going to drink?" "You only want water? Are you sure?" "Why aren't you drinking. This day is important to me. We're celebrating (insert event here)." And so on.

It means I am feeling completely disconnected and don't want people to continually ask me, "What's wrong? You look upset. Everything okay?" When in fact, everything is fine, I am just experiencing a common lack of emotion that leaves me appearing and feeling emotionless and uncaring.

It means I am feeling particularly paranoid or self-conscious. I pay too much attention to everyone's facial expressions and body language, then misinterpret them in order to self-sabotage my personal growth and positive feelings. I will then behave emotional and quiet, leading everyone to ask, "Is everything okay?" repeatedly, which will result in me crying and making a scene.

It means that I am desperate to have friends, but know people get tired of offering to only hear me say no, again. It means I know my emotions are complicated and I bring people in and then push them away. It means that even though I seem at times annoying, irrational, distant, or snobby, that's really not the case.

It means I know you have found me funny, loyal, always willing to help someone out, sensitive yet a straight shooter. I appreciate you for finding some quality in me you liked and hope you will find some understanding to the depths of my illness. Reach out, and if I decline, say "Okay, next time." But also, be able to say, "You know what, this is important to me, and I really want you to come."

Sincerely,

Your friend, Rivka

TWENTY

Marriage

My husband and I could not be any more different. In our house it's often Yankee versus the South, liberal versus conservative, Baptist versus Jewish, Buddha and universal energies, rigid versus go with the flow, hoarding versus minimalism, and masculine ego versus feminine power. In any combination on any given day. Sprinkled with dysfunctional responses created from our past environments. Some days it's downright comical and others a battle of the wills.

There are numerous books for someone married to a person with a mental illness to purchase and study. There is very little in the reverse. Intensive therapy is often the only outlet to combat the high statistics for failed marriage, not only in general, but with mental illness at the helm. It's not just up to my husband to learn to tiptoe around my erratic existence, to learn to communicate with me better, notice signs of change, oversee medication is taken, while processing what I say and do without internalizing the blows.

It is unfair to put that enormous burden on him. Our statistic for divorce is by far greater than most. Each with multiple failed marriages, his line of work, coupled with my bipolar disorder. Being medicated and stable doesn't equate too easy. In fact, it's harder. Previously unscathed by the departure of yet another failed nuptial, I'm now cognizant of every factor looming over our success or demise. Like the awakening during our vows, I am clear for once. I have to learn to be a partner, unselfish, dedicated, compromising, loyal, passionate, and gracious.

If I am still responding to the world around me as if the world is my mother and I am twelve years old , combative, selfish, careless with my words, and disconnected, I fail to communicate in a healthy way. Additionally, if I also hold on to past unrealistic expectations, I will also put them on my husband and children. Primarily materialistic ones. To set this aside is something I have been unable to do for the majority of my life. This is no easy task

In my discovery and self-care, my husband and I share a mutual understanding, an agreement, to decide that even with all the obstacles, we choose each other. It is patience tenfold. It is grace and forgiveness in abundance. It is constantly learning and growing, even if it's not simultaneously. It is slamming a door in his face one day and looking him in the eye the next day determined in my commitment. It is his misunderstandings and gruff tone one day, and apologetic affection the next. There is an ebb and flow, but with us the shifts are heightened by our circumstances. If that doesn't make us a power couple, I don't know what does.

To all the therapists I quit,

You probably don't remember me, but I will never forget each of you. I humbly thank you for being a voice, even if only for a fleeting moment. Each of you contributed something of value to my battle. Each of you, in your own creative desire, offered and encouraged insight and your wisdom on how I can maintain a sense of self during the worst of times. You left a lasting impact on my life.

You taught me S.T.O.P., the stop, think, observe, and plan acronym. You taught me creative ways to expel aggression, such as purchasing old plates from garage sales and use them to throw at a strung-up sheet in my garage, tagging each one with something or someone emotionally holding back. Throwing each one with an exuberant force while letting out any shame, guilt, insecurities, grief, and rejection with it.

You taught me the love of journaling and writing in the most cathartic way. You gave me ways to remain positive and parent effectively after each destructive mania or debilitating depression. You showed me how to love myself the best I possibly can even if I felt I would never experience society's idea of normal.

You chose a modest profession. I may not have acknowledged you then—you may have thought I wasn't taking you seriously or maybe I even seemed ungrateful—but I promise you, each little golden trinket of knowledge and advice was captured permanently in my subconscious to be utilized when I was emotionally ready to hear it. Each of you took me in at my worst. You never judged me or condemned me as I condemned myself. Without each of you I wouldn't have made it to where I am now: with a good relationship with my children intact, and the ability to accept the love I deserve. I would not have continued to fight for my place in this universe.

Forever grateful,

Rivka

And every woman who continues to fight and seek your help at their own pace.

TWENTY ONE

In the Now

During a session at intensive outpatient therapy, we focused on a lesson of mindfulness. The concept sounded lovely and unrealistic. Given a worksheet with seventy-one ways to practice mindfulness, I realized there are in fact a few things on this list I enjoy. Not just enjoy but love. Things I have become out of touch with that bring a sense of peacefulness just thinking about them.

Number twenty-one, connect with nature. Number fifty-eight, practice walking meditation. Accompanied by a list of ninety-seven additional coping skills. Number one, listen to music. Number fifteen, write poetry. Number eighty-five, be with nature. Outpatient therapy comes with a myriad of ways to instill coping mechanisms. Skills I initiated as a child to find and create some peace.

My husband and I moved to a six-acre, semi-wooded piece of land with a hundred-year-old farmhouse. This farmhouse was an exciting notion of a creative endeavor. One that brought about feelings of teamwork in inventing our dream home nestled in the quiet country.

This was not the dream that took place. With my often-declining moods and an extreme hypersensitivity to disorganization and chaos, this project turned into a nightmare.

With the coping skills, a rekindled appreciation, and love for nature, I was able to reset my thinking about the country setting around me. I walk the perimeter taking in the scents, the sounds, the colors of the landscape, and envision the home we intend to create. Taking up mindful walking brings back that childlike sense of peacefulness.

I created an area for myself luring me to relaxation. A hammock is strung from the trees, a rough stone fire pit nearby, a table and chairs under the shade of a large oak tree, and twinkle lights surround the outdoor living space. I sip my coffee at the table and watch the sunrise while the barn cats visit. During the day the table is my outdoor office, while the hammock is where I take my breaks. The surrounding trees offer shade and hold a soft breeze. It's rustic and reminiscent of a campsite.

After a short reprieve, I rekindled my love for journaling. Not just journaling, but reading books, writing down all of my ideas and notions. Having never been a poetic person before, I find myself lyrically putting together thoughts and feelings, creating a deep emotional response. After a walk, I enjoy recalling what I saw and putting it to pen. It's a reminder of those positive feelings put to paper. Something you can refer back to when you are down or unable to go outside. It is truly rewarding to actually feel how good it is to self-manage in a healthy way.

On a more creative side I took up photography. Nature photography is where my keen eye finds the most beauty, although I love taking action photos of my youngest son and daughter's rugby matches. I am quite surprised at my work to date. Me, taking photos of Mother nature's raw and fascinating life or the athleticism of my children is very cathartic. Once again, being with nature, at least for me, has an almost instantaneously positive response. I can walk it, write about it, photograph it, and incorporate it into my life through any circumstances.

I've clearly found my coping skills, mindfullness and everything tied in nature. It was an environmental or biological provided source for a defense mechanism. As if God or the universe was preparing me for my hardships. After my parents split, I was shown Doug's farm. And in each subsequent area of my life, deep scenic nature was just around the corner. Always waiting, always inviting me back, always calling me home. Music is also beneficial. It can literally change a mood for the better and even for the worse. If you want a partner in your sadness, music can offer that friendship. If you want a beat to mirror your excitement, it won't let you down. Need to scream off some rage? There is a song for that too. There's even music to share in my quiet admiration of nature.

What is your coping skill? What do you think the universe was telling you all along? If not in nature, music, or meditation, is it tapping, counting, a bag of fidget devices? I learned of a woman in one of my groups who carried a stress bag. Inside was an essential oil, a worry stone, crystals, and personal items of some significance. In times of severe panic I like to use another approach. I say out loud everything

I see around me in great detail. Brown chair made with hardwood. Laminate floor with a black and white pattern, old and creased. Window to my left, with white curtains and so on. I do this until that ball of emotion in my chest dissipates.

Find what works for you, hone in on it, make adjustments, and know that what you choose is unique to you. There is no one-coping-skill-fits-all approach here. But before you do, make sure you come to terms with where you've been, what you've done, where you are now, and where you see yourself going. Be patient in finding your medication lottery. Utilize as much therapy as you need. Don't limit yourself because of your illness. Don't limit yourself because everyone up until now told you otherwise. You are not your illness; you are what you've become because of it. Let that define your strength and successes. Put your monsters away. You're stronger than they are now.

A NOTE FROM THE AUTHOR

In all I've learned over the years, in all the changes I have made, and in all the ways I have created an environment more conducive to my well-being, life happens. It throws curveballs. Some so deviated from your course, you may have to set a new one. How we manage that will set a precedent going forward. This is *me* telling *you* you can do it.

Just weeks into completing this book, I was given distressing news. Early into my writings I talk about malformed lens fibers in utero. This is in reference to my right eye. I was born with a rare posterior cataract. Also referred to as a trauma cataract. There is no definitive reason for this; sometimes it happens in the womb and sometimes by forceps during childbirth.

As a result, a secondary condition occurred called amblyopia. In common terms, this means lazy eye. But in my case, this means a disconnect between my bad eye and my brain. They don't work together in order to attempt any vision correction. Instead, my brain favors only my functioning left eye. This condition didn't cause any considerable limitations in school or at home. In fact, I barely acknowledged its existence. I was able to pass my driver's exam, and receive a document from an eye doctor in order to pass their visual requirements. I even talked my way through the military visual assessments and later again in basic training.

Having a primarily blind eye makes the functioning eye coveted with every hint of blurriness immediately noticeable. Which is exactly what took place just a month prior to my father's passing. My opthalmologist requested an OCT (optical coherence tomography) test to determine if there were any retinal issues, such as macular degeneration or diabetic retinopathy. What he found was an indication of macular changes eluding to some type of retinal disease. I was promptly sent to a retina specialist to determine the scope of this abnormality.

After a fluorescein angiogram was performed to see the blood vessels behind the retina or any other fluid-like macular changes, I was diagnosed with a condition called CSR (central serous retinopathy). This is a fluid buildup in the macular area behind the retina. The only known related cause is corticosteroids or stress and potentially some underlying medical conditions to which I do not have.

The good news for most is CSR is self-healing over time and rarely returns. For some, it does, and in that case options such as laser treatments and eye injections can be offered. There is a small percentage of people who experience a more serious version, treatment resistant or chronic. I have had one laser procedure and one injection.

Five years has come to pass and I have significantly diminished vision and continually chronic fluid leaks.

A new specialist is attempting a new laser treatment option called photodynamic therapy with no guarantee. This leaves me with a potentially blinding scenario. I am already learning to focus on what I hear when I'm relaxing in the hammock. How the sun feels on my face. How my feet feel grounded in the grass. And how I can adjust my coping skills to serve a possible new existence.

Do not let setbacks alter your course. Always have a contingency plan for moments unexpected. Let no one and nothing stop you from winning the war for dominance over your own mental existence. In the past, I doubt I would have survived such a blow. But there is a pride in how far I've come. And with that pride comes a sense of strength. I will falter, I will have moments of weakness, but I am at a new level of consciousness. My story is unique, and it will always end in my control over my monsters, with sight or blind. I am not afraid.

Love to each of you,
Tell your story now.
Rivka Stieh

A tribute to my father, who grew up during the Depression living out of cars and tents. Despite the odds he became one of the most honored Missouri state senators to date. Your story is next dad.

The Senator

I'm a big boy, mama, I'm gonna help us through
We live in a one-bedroom house for more than me and you
No work, no money, and no food
But the car is roomy, it's got big seats
It'll only be temporary until we find some work and eats
Took my napsack and tied it to my waist
Gonna get some work and send home money, no time to waste
I'll climb into dark shadows where the birds don't sing
My face and blue overalls stained from the sorrow this job brings
I got some change in my pocket now it's time to move on
I'm the man now, mama, take this money and hang on
I'm headed to Korea, I'm gonna be fine
Bringing home the soldier's dollar to care of mines
I've got some change in my pocket, now it's time to move on
I'm a man now, mama, take this money and hang on
I'll cut, weld, paint, and farm until my fingers bleed
I'll always be here to take care of what you need
This is only temporary, your expectations I'll exceed
Someday I'm gonna change things
So future families may never see the suffering such poverty can bring

If you or someone you know is experiencing a mental crisis, suicidal thoughts, or suffering from physical and mental abuse or addiction please contact one of the available resources I am providing here. In situations of abuse, going to your local emergency room can also offer immediate intervention. These National resources can provide immediate assistance while providing local contacts.

You are not alone.

National Suicide Prevention Lifeline: 800-273-8255

NAMI (National Alliance on Mental Illness): 800-950-6264

National Domestic Violence Hotline: 800-787-3224

The Trevor Project, National organization for LGBTQ crisis intervention: 866-488-7386

NEDA (National Eating Disorder Helpline): 800-931-2237 call or text

National Coalition for the Homeless: 800-621-4000

National Runaway Safeline: Local 211 hotline or 800-621-4000

Safe Place Sign Locations for Youth: Go to the location of the sign, ask for help, the store location will put you in a safe place until a qualified Safe Place volunteer or agency staff member will arrive to bring you to safety. You may also text TXT 4 HELP (44357) to receive information about the closest Safe Place location.

Made in the USA
Monee, IL
20 July 2023

39307287R00115